2-63

CONSTITUTION MAKING IN ILLINOIS, 1818–1970

STUDIES IN ILLINOIS CONSTITUTION MAKING
Joseph P. Pisciotte, *Editor*

Constitution Making in Illinois
1818–1970

JANET CORNELIUS

Published for the
INSTITUTE OF GOVERNMENT AND PUBLIC AFFAIRS
by the
UNIVERSITY OF ILLINOIS PRESS
Urbana   Chicago   London

*Special appreciation is expressed to
the Field Foundation of Illinois,
whose financial support has made
this series possible.*

© 1972 by The Board of Trustees of the University of Illinois
Manufactured in the United States of America
Library of Congress Catalog No. 72-76864

ISBN 0-252-00251-2

Contents

Foreword

An increasing number of academic and participant observers are becoming sharply aware of the absence of a significant body of literature dealing with the processes of state constitutional revision. Awareness of this void has quickened recently as citizens and governmental officials in more and more states have taken an interest in various forms of constitutional revision.

The National Municipal League has led the field in developing what literature does exist, but even their efforts — a valuable beginning — have dealt only with such topics as the need for reform and the means of effecting constitutional revision once the need is realized. Recently, while continuing to serve as a clearinghouse of information, the League has gone a step further and sponsored individual studies of most of the state constitutional conventions since 1940. These studies fall into the same category as most of the other writings on state constitutional revision, that is, they are descriptive and analytic and reflect the viewpoint of only one observer. In each instance the reader is forced to accept the conclusions of one writer using one particular method of analysis.

Many still feel the need for more probing analyses to deal with questions which are answered now mostly by speculation. For example, we know very little about the impact of demographic variables, urbanization, or party on the outcome of elections required to initiate or implement revisions. We are not certain as to the advantages or disadvantages of partisan versus nonpartisan conventions. We are unsure about how best to organize and operate conventions, and to present a proposed change to the voters. We have yet to analyze fully alternative methods of selecting public officials and the resulting outputs of the agency or department involved, and most importantly, we have not yet begun accurately to assess the role of constitutional reform in state government and politics. Although we generally accept the premise that reform is needed, we are not certain of its impact, if any, on social and political change. Some have argued that constitutional reform is more symbolic than substantive, and that its effect is determined by other forces at work on decision making in state and local government.

The recently concluded Sixth Illinois Constitutional Convention provided observers an excellent opportunity to study the constitutional revision process. The Institute of Government and Public Affairs of the University of Illinois has authorized the writing and publication of a series of monographs, Studies in Illinois Constitution Making, which examine the Illinois convention and attempt to deal with some of the unanswered questions about state constitutional revision. Each study treats a specific phase of the revision process and is written by authors who had a close relationship to the convention in one of several capacities. The studies display a variety of methodologies in their analyses and conclusions.

The primary aim of the series is to recount — in breadth and detail — the events, personalities, strategies, conflicts, and resolutions which resulted in a new basic law for Illinois. Neither the convention nor these studies were conducted in isolation from the political environment of the state, hence, the first of several secondary goals of the series is to contribute to the general knowledge of the politics of Illinois. It is also our aim to provide a basis for later studies dealing with the implementation and impact of the new document. And finally, it is our hope that the series will lend itself to comparative studies on state constitutional revision and ultimately to the development of descriptive and theoretical literature in this area.

The Institute expresses its deep appreciation to the Field Foundation of Illinois which recognized the need for these studies and provided the funding for them. In each study the statements and views expressed are solely the responsibility of the author.

JOSEPH P. PISCIOTTE
Series Editor
SAMUEL K. GOVE
Institute Director

Preface

Constitution Making in Illinois, 1818–1970 is a revised edition of *A History of Constitution Making in Illinois,* which I prepared in 1968 for the Constitution Study Commission of the Seventy-fifth General Assembly under the auspices of the Institute of Government and Public Affairs of the University of Illinois. The original edition, issued in a multilith printing, was intended as a survey of Illinois constitutions and constitutional conventions for the information of the general public. It was also used by the delegates to the Sixth Illinois Constitutional Convention in 1969. As its purpose was to provide the general reader with some background on previous constitutional developments in Illinois, the first edition is not an entirely new work of primary scholarship, but rather a survey of information on constitutional revision from both primary and secondary sources.

The present work is directly descended from the original edition — though completely revised. Many aspects of Illinois constitution making have been explored in greater depth, particularly in the period after 1870, while a few have been condensed. Where good secondary sources were available they have been used. I have placed more stress on comparisons with other state constitutions, and have attempted to deal with the question of the purpose and significance of constitutions in the political life of a state. I have also added a new chapter surveying the Illinois constitutional convention of 1969–70 in its relationship to previous constitution making in the state. It is my hope that the reader will be stimulated by the parallels and contrasts in Illinois constitution making during a span of 158 years to ask himself some basic questions: What is the real position and purpose of state constitutions, and further, what does state constitutional development have to indicate about the relationship of the American people to their systems of written law?

Many people have given aid and advice during the preparation of this work. I would particularly like to thank Professors Wallace Farnham and Robert M. Sutton of the University of Illinois for their reading of the manuscript in preparation and their helpful suggestions for improvement, and Illinois State Historian William Alterfer for also reading and commenting on the manuscript. Samuel Witwer, president of the 1969–70 constitutional convention, very kindly gave his valuable time for a recorded interview on his interpretation of that convention. Joseph Pisciotte, professor at the Institute of Government and executive director of the 1969–70 convention, also provided information on the convention, as well as inspiration and encouragement as series editor. Credit is also due Richard J. Carlson who wrote the first draft of chapter VI and J. D. Bindenagel who spent hours in the library running down sources, checking footnotes, and preparing the index. Ashley Nugent gave the manuscript careful and skillful editing, and the secretarial staff at the Institute — Jean Baker, Loretta McKeighen, and Lorena McClain — twice turned a rough draft into a manuscript. Ultimately, of course, I am responsible for any errors and deficiencies in the book.

JANET CORNELIUS

Introduction

While the concept of a higher law, binding on ruler and ruled alike, has found expression at intervals in most of recorded history, the *written* constitution is of relatively recent origin and is essentially an American invention. Although scholars differ on the ideal form, there is general agreement that a constitution is an accepted body of organic laws which structures the government of a state; limits the powers of the legislative, executive, and judicial branches; and guarantees the rights, immunities, and liberties of the people. Such a constitution can exist and indeed be effective though not reduced to writing, as demonstrated by the experiences of England and other nations which have *unwritten* constitutions. In fact, the reduction of constitutional ideas to writing, Magna Carta and several ancient legal codes notwithstanding, has been the exceptional practice, not the rule.

But Americans see a constitution as something which should rest upon a more certain basis than tradition, custom, and precedent. From the earliest days of the American experiment in government, the notion that the higher law should be written law became a fundamental pillar of our political system. Since the signing in 1620 of the Mayflower Compact, the colonies and, in turn, all of our states and the federal government adopted written formulations, stating what it was that a government might or might not do and defining what was meant by the inalienable rights of its citizens.

By inherent nature, unwritten constitutions evolve slowly, but they also evolve continuously, affording some degree of adaptability to changing needs. On the other hand, the process of adopting or

revising written constitutions is episodic. Particularly when the "reduction to writing" phase leads to excessive detail and wordiness the
result can be marked constitutional rigidity which can be overcome
only by an enlightened use of a workable amending article in the
document itself.

Another distinctive characteristic of American constitution making
has been its high degree of citizen involvement. Every American
state constitution, save one, expressly recognizes that all political
power is derived from the people, affirming the words of the Declaration of Independence that "to secure these rights . . . governments
are instituted among men deriving their just powers from the consent of the governed." The New York Constitution, the exception,
clearly implies it. Implementing this cardinal belief concerning the
source of political power are procedures in practically all states, involving people at every stage of constitution making. The chosen
vehicle has been another American innovation, the constitutional
convention. Almost uniformly such conventions are "called" or convened by vote of the people. Then citizen-delegates are elected by
the people to draft the fundamental law. In time the work product
of the convention is submitted to the people for ratification. Such
constitutional conventions have been the principal means utilized in
writing new organic laws and revising the old, and to date the states
have held more than two hundred conventions. Citizen participation
is equally basic in adopting legislatively initiated constitutional
amendments, this process likewise requiring voter approval. American constitutions are indeed people's documents.

Justice Cardozo once wrote, "A constitution states, or ought to
state, not rules for the passing hour, but principles for an expanding
future." The 1870 Illinois Constitution was not so drafted. It was
deliberately fashioned so as to shackle the hands of those entrusted
with public authority, reflecting the then popular distrust of the executive, legislative, and judicial departments of government. It was
weighed down with detail and provisions customarily found in
statutes and ordinances. It embodied not only the wise federal system of checks and balances but also an inner structure of checks and
balances. Above all, it was written to meet the needs of a rural and
agrarian society, not our present complex urbanized and industrial-
ized community. Tremendous changes have occurred in the inter-

vening years including a depression of world-wide magnitude, global wars of unsurpassed destruction, revolutionary advances in communications, transportation, and technology, vast changes in the scope and character of public education, the coming of the Atomic Age, major migrations of populations from rural to urban to suburban areas, the growth of huge cities and in turn their partial obsolescence, to mention but a few. Most of the vexing problems now confronting every branch of state and local government relate to one or more of these developments.

Yet, with the exception of the judicial branch of government, which underwent reorganization following adoption of the Judicial Amendment in 1962, Illinois's basic government remained static from 1870 to 1970. This was due to the state's feeble ability to amend or revise its constitution of 1870 except on relatively rare occasions. Contrary to Illinois's experience in the nineteenth century, the people of this century have had but limited chance to reshape their constitutional law by the convention method. There had been one convention since 1870, and the revisions proposed by that convention were decisively rejected in 1922.

Prior to adoption of the so-called Gateway amendment in 1950, the revision of the constitution in a piecemeal manner seemed equally unattainable. All efforts in that regard after 1908 had failed largely because of the large number of voters who went to the polls at general elections and failed to vote on the constitutional amendments proposed. Under court rulings they were counted, in effect, as "no" voters in determining whether a particular amendment had been approved by "a majority of the electors voting at the said election," the referendum requirement of Article XIV of the constitution. The chapter of this study concerning developments after the adoption of Gateway wisely deals with a critical period in the history of Illinois constitution making. While it is true that little change in substantive constitutional law, other than the judicial amendment, was achieved in the twenty years which followed adoption of the Gateway amendment, the numerous blue ballot campaigns were of crucial importance in setting the stage for the successful convention call of 1968. By means of those campaigns, involving an unprecedented unity of effort by political leadership, most major farm, labor, business, and civic organizations, the mass media and thousands of dedicated citizens, the state was for the first time alerted to the inadequacies of its obsolescent constitution and the critical need for its prompt revision. Moreover, until reapportionment of the state's senatorial districts, from which the constitutional convention delegates are chosen, any proposal to call a convention would have encountered strenuous urban opposition. Not until after the invoking of the one man, one vote principle by the courts was this roadblock to a convention overcome.

A significant contribution of this history, as originally prepared for the Illinois Constitution Study Commission, was the light it threw on the quality and type of convention which had to be held in 1970 if Illinois were to have a modern and serviceable constitution. The account of the 1869–70 constitutional convention and subsequent developments made clear the costs to a state when organic law is written with prolixity and in excessive detail. Similarly, the interesting accounts of the unsuccessful conventions of 1862 and 1920–22 demonstrated the futility of expecting a soundly drafted constitution to emerge from an unsoundly structured convention. History in Illinois and elsewhere has shown that conventions torn with partisan or sectional strife, or controlled by or submissive to any interest other than the broad public interest, have little chance of success. Those state constitutional conventions which have viewed their function to be essentially legislative, which have dealt with the immediately pressing or only transiently significant issues of government or public policy, seldom have been successful in securing ratification of their work or in drafting constitutions of excellence and distinction.

Twenty-five years ago, the late Kenneth C. Sears, a leading constitutional scholar whose studies have been greatly influential in bringing about needed constitutional reform, declared: "Illinois, everything considered, is in the worst position of any state of the Union." This charge is no longer valid.

That Illinois now has adopted a new constitution far better than the old, both in meeting present needs and in adherence to classic standards of constitution writing, can scarcely be questioned. Many political scientists and students of constitutional government already have spoken highly of the new constitution. Some have acclaimed its adoption as a monumental achievement in the context of the failures which have been encountered in this century in other American states.

But in the last analysis, the final qualitative judgment depends upon and must await the outcome of legislative implementation and judicial interpretation. I feel that there is good reason to assume that these two will be accomplished with distinction and in a manner fulfilling the hopes and aspirations of an overwhelming majority of Illinois citizens when they adopted their constitution of 1970.

SAMUEL W. WITWER
President, Sixth Illinois
Constitutional Convention

CONSTITUTION MAKING IN ILLINOIS, 1818–1970

County Boundaries and Settled Places in Illinois, 1818

1818 COUNTIES

1. Bond
2. Crawford
3. Edwards
4. Franklin
5. Gallatin
6. Jackson
7. Johnson
8. Madison
9. Monroe
10. Pope
11. Randolph
12. St. Clair
13. Union
14. Washington
15. White

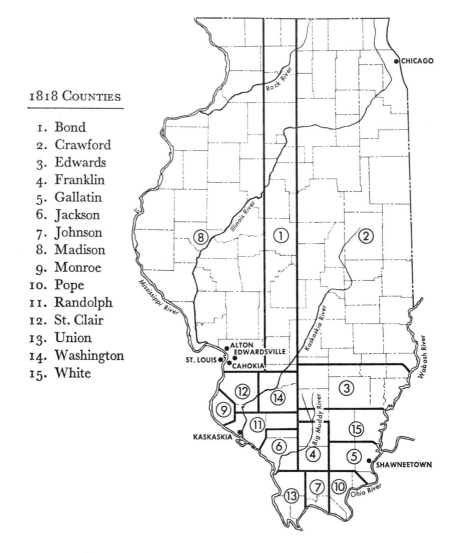

I

The Frontier Constitution

In December 1817 the legislature of the Territory of Illinois petitioned the United States Congress for permission to take the required steps leading to statehood. At the time the population of the territory had not yet been officially established at sixty thousand, the number suggested for statehood by the Northwest Ordinance, or even thirty-five thousand, the ratio of Congressional apportionment at the time. Inhabitants of Illinois were concentrated in the lower third of the territory, along the Mississippi and Wabash-Ohio rivers — concentrated, however, only to the extent of reaching a population density of eight to the square mile in some areas. In small numbers and scattered settlements, and with varied backgrounds, interests, and ambitions, the inhabitants of Illinois could not organize to promote their territory's becoming a state. Instead, one man, Daniel Pope Cook, capitalized on the popular desire for statehood to further his own political ambition.

MOVEMENT FOR STATEHOOD

Cook's efforts appeared promising for several reasons. Illinois settlers were dissatisfied with their colonial status in a territory administered according to the Northwest Ordinance of 1787, and had early shown a desire for autonomy. As part of Indiana Territory they had been frustrated by Governor William Henry Harrison's policies of appointing most officials from Indiana sections of the

3

territory, and irritated by a Harrison appointee's controversial investigations into fraudulent land claims perpetrated by many of Illinois's most prominent citizens. Therefore in 1809 an organized minority of Illinois settlers had brought about the establishment of Illinois as a separate territory. Further insistence by Illinois residents in 1812 prompted Governor Ninian Edwards to ask Congress to allow Illinois the next step toward statehood as provided for in the Northwest Ordinance — the election of a territorial legislature. The voters chose a delegate to Congress, a council of five to assist the governor, and a house of representatives consisting of six legislators.[1]

One of the first acts of this legislature was to attempt to improve a serious defect of territorial government — the administration of justice in the territory. Particularly onerous were Illinois's three federally-appointed judges, who neglected their duties and were absent from the territory for long periods of time. The legislature tried to specify how and when the judges should hold sessions, but the judges, led by Justice Jesse B. Thomas fought back while Governor Edwards supported the legislature. When even Congressional legislation failed to regulate the judges' activities, the legislature gave up, established local law courts at the territory's expense, and let the judges alone, except for the calling of four general courts each year. Clearly the position of these territorial judges was a sore point with the settlers, and a problem which would be alleviated by statehood.[2]

Another irritant to the settlers was the position of the governor, also federally-appointed from outside the territory. Ninian Edwards of Kentucky had performed a creditable job in mitigating previous factionalism in Illinois, but his appointments had inevitably aroused resentment from those passed over as well as from Thomas's judicial faction. Also strongly resented was the provision of the Ordinance of 1787 which gave certain legislative powers to the governor, and which was interpreted by territorial governors as a grant of absolute

[1] For thorough discussions of Illinois's territorial government, see the introduction in Francis S. Philbrick, ed., *The Laws of Indiana Territory, 1801–1809, Collections of the Illinois State Historical Library* 21 (Springfield, 1930) ; introduction in Philbrick, ed., *Laws of the Illinois Territory, 1809–1818,* ibid. 25 (Springfield, 1950) ; Clarence Alvord, *The Illinois Country, 1673–1818* (Chicago: Loyola University Press Reprint Series, 1965) ; and Solon J. Buck, *Illinois in 1818,* 2d ed. rev. (Urbana: University of Illinois Press, 1967), originally published as the introductory volume of The Centennial History of Illinois.

[2] Alvord, pp. 432–33.

veto power over any measures passed by the elected territorial legislatures. This seemed to the settlers to be a travesty of representative
government and an intrusion on their political rights. It was a measure which only statehood could correct.

Ironically, though, it was Governor Edwards's protegee, Cook,
nephew of Congressional delegate Nathaniel Pope, who sparked the
movement for statehood. Acquiring an interest in the *Western Intelligencer,* the territory's only newspaper, Cook wrote several articles
pointing out that Illinois's difficulties would be straightened out once
she became a state. Governor Edwards suggested that a census be
taken as a first step in the process, but the territorial legislators, led
by Cook, decided not to wait. They appointed a committee to draft
a memorial to Congress requesting Illinois's admission as a state.[3]

This haste seemed necessary. Settlers were pouring into Illinois
after land offices had opened in 1814 and 1816 and choice locations
in Ohio, Indiana, and Kentucky had filled up; in 1818 less than
half its settlers had lived in Illinois three years, and less than a third
had been residents for as long as ten years. Settlement continually
advanced faster than land sales, and settlers hoped that statehood
would speed up the tedious process of settling private claims and
opening land for purchase.

Events elsewhere also stimulated Illinois's haste. Indiana had become a state in 1816 and Mississippi in 1817, and in 1818 Missouri
was preparing petitions for statehood. Illinois, further east, wanted
the prestige of attaining statehood before Missouri; also, there was
the problem of the status of slavery in Illinois.

The Northwest Ordinance of 1787 had prohibited slavery, but
Illinois had been a county of Virginia, and when Virginia ceded
Illinois to the United States in 1784, it did so on condition that
the inhabitants would have "their possessions and titles [including
slaves] confirmed to them." Since many of the old French settlers
did own slaves, the Northwest Ordinance was interpreted as forbidding only the future introduction of slaves. Then in 1805 and 1807
territorial legislatures passed laws binding whole families of blacks
to long terms as "indentured servants" in the territory.[4]

This equivocal situation was exacerbated by the westward move-

[3] Buck, *Illinois in 1818,* pp. 211–13.
[4] Ibid., p. 187.

ment of the American population. The early Illinois settlers from English North America came from the southern plantation areas and were disposed to continue the slave labor system. However, the newer settlers from Kentucky and Tennessee were experienced pioneers, characterized more as westerners than southerners, and were joined by increasing numbers from Ohio and New England and by immigrants from the British Isles. Many of the new settlers did not favor, and a few vigorously opposed, the extension of slavery in Illinois.

Both proponents and opponents of slavery wanted to develop the state and attract settlers. With slavery neither totally prohibited nor fully allowed both sides hoped they might prevail. Those favoring the repeal of the slavery prohibition disliked seeing wealthy slaveholders pass through Illinois to settle in Missouri, which was likely soon to become a slave state. Antislavery men felt Illinois would prosper without the institution but might be tempted to allow it if Missouri achieved statehood first and prospered under the slave system.

For these reasons Illinois raced Missouri to statehood. Missouri began her movement for statehood a month or two earlier, but Congress passed an enabling bill for Illinois's constitutional convention first, and President Monroe signed it April 18, 1818. The people of the territory were to elect thirty-three delegates in July who would convene in August. Illinois would become a state before Missouri if it produced evidence of a population of forty thousand and then a constitution acceptable to the United States Congress.[5]

ELECTION OF DELEGATES

Little is known of the campaign for the election of delegates except from letters written to the *Intelligencer* during the campaign; judging from these letters, the slavery question played an important part

---

[5] The enabling act is reprinted in Emil J. Verlie, ed., *Illinois Constitutions, Collections of the Illinois State Historical Library* 13 (Springfield, 1919):15–19. The memorial from the territorial legislature to Congress requested Illinois's admission as a state with a population of 40,000. Although there was some feeling that Illinois should have the 60,000 population suggested by the Ordinance of 1787, Congress acquiesced, and the enabling act contained the figure 40,000. Buck, *Illinois in 1818*, pp. 227–28, 309, reviews the apportionment for delegates.

in the selection of delegates. A May 27 letter signed "The People" said that "the object which most interests the public mind, with regard to the approaching election for members to the convention, is to know whether they are in favor of the toleration or the prohibition of slavery."[6] The extreme proslavery men said little in print in support of their cause, but an examination of the retorts of the antislavery writers suggests that the proslavery arguments stressed the greater revenue Illinois would gain from rich slaveholders. The part slavery played in the selection of delegates from some areas became evident during the convention when the representatives of Union, Johnson, and Edwards counties constantly voted on the antislavery side in convention issues, and the Gallatin, Randolph, and Jackson county representatives voted consistently for the recognition of indentured servitude and slavery in Illinois.[7]

There is no evidence that political parties were a factor in the campaign, although two factions which were to play a large part in the politics of Illinois for the next decades were already forming.[8] Apart from the slavery issue, personalities and campaign techniques played the largest part in determining the candidates selected. A wide personal acquaintance in his area was necessary for a delegate's candidacy, and campaigning was largely carried on by door-to-door canvassing. This may explain why three doctors, with their wide circles of acquaintance were elected to the convention, and suggests why five of the fifteen commissioners taking the census during the campaign became delegates to the convention.[9]

The method of voting for convention delegates on July 6, 7, and 8 was viva voce; the vote of each elector was recorded and proclaimed aloud by his county sheriff. The viva voce system had been substituted for written ballots by the territorial legislature in 1813, both to avoid embarrassing those who had not learned to read and write and to prevent bribery and corruption by "electioneering

[6] *Illinois Intelligencer,* May 27, 1818.

[7] Buck, *Illinois in 1818,* pp. 256–57.

[8] Ibid., p. 233. One group was led by Ninian Edwards, Nathaniel Pope, Daniel Pope Cook, General Leonard White, and Judge Thomas Browne, and the other was led by Shadrach Bond, Jesse B. Thomas, Michael Jones, Elias Kent Kane, and others. The campaign for delegates does not seem to have been a contest between these two groups, although the second faction was more prominent in forming the constitution. Ibid., p. 201.

[9] Ibid., p. 258.

zealots," even though it was pointed out during the convention campaign that the viva voce system was even more conducive to bribery and corruption.[10] Records of the vote for delegates are available only for Madison County, and even these are open to question. According to these records, there were 1,012 men of voting age in the county at the time of the election. A total of 517 votes was cast for delegates in Madison County. This is a creditable turnout since many who voted probably did not meet the six-month residence requirement, and many had a long way to travel to the only voting center in the county.[11]

Complete information on the backgrounds of the delegates is unavailable, but a glance at their known occupations shows a frontier versatility. Many of them were employed in two or three occupations; most numbered farming as one. Only five delegates had legal training, and three of these were judges in the territory. The convention members included three physicians, a flatboater, two sheriffs, a minister, a storekeeper, and a land office official. At least four delegates were connected with the salt industry, which was worked almost entirely by slave labor. The convention was the beginning or continuation of a political career for many: three members had been in the territorial legislature which petitioned for statehood, including the speaker, Dr. George Fisher, and at least twenty of the thirty-three delegates were elected to state office in the years after the convention.[12]

The two most prominent members of the convention were un-

[10] *Illinois Intelligencer*, July 1, 1818.

[11] Buck, *Illinois in 1818*, p. 260. At that time Madison County had its present southern boundaries, but its northern and western boundaries extended to the present northern and western state lines. However, only in the three southern tiers of townships could land be purchased before 1819, and the extreme edge of frontier settlement was delineated at Macoupin Creek, across present Jersey and Calhoun counties, to the Mississippi River. Ibid., p. 82.

[12] "The Illinois Constitutional Convention of 1818," *Journal of the Illinois State Historical Society* 6 (1913):327–424. This includes the *Journal of the Convention* (Kaskaskia, 1818), an introduction by Richard V. Carpenter, and notes by J. W. Kitchell. Subsequent references will be made to Carpenter's introduction and to the journal, and the page numbers given will be those in the state historical society article.

The information on the delegates is from Carpenter, pp. 330–47. Five of the thirty-three delegates gave their names to counties in the new state. These were Benjamin Stephenson, Elias Kent Kane, Conrad Will, General Leonard White, and William McHenry.

doubtedly Jesse B. Thomas and Elias Kent Kane. Thomas typified the older leaders of the territory in origin and career. He was born at Hagerstown, Maryland, and claimed direct descent from Lord Baltimore. An attorney, he settled first in Indiana Territory in 1803, served as an Indiana delegate to Congress, and led an anti-Harrison faction which sought to separate Illinois from Indiana. He was appointed one of the first territorial judges when Illinois Territory was organized in 1809, and became one of the leaders of the anti-Edwards faction in the new territory. Thomas was president of the constitutional convention in 1818 and was subsequently elected to the United States Senate where in 1820 he introduced the Missouri Compromise.[13]

Elias Kent Kane was representative of the newer type of Illinois politician, the young, ambitious lawyer recently come to the territory with the hope of finding there the road to wealth and prominence. Kane was born in New York and educated at Yale College. In 1814 he moved to Kaskaskia to practice law and was appointed a territorial judge early in 1818. He had considerable influence in drawing up the constitution of 1818 and served as the first secretary of state under the new state government. From 1824 until his death in 1835, he served as United States Senator.[14]

Although the convention counted among its members a person claiming to have been the first white born in Illinois, Enoch Moore of Washington County, most of the delegates had immigrated to the territory. A division in the geographical origin of Illinois settlers was mirrored in delegate origins: nine delegates came from the southern states of Kentucky, Tennessee, and Virginia, and six from the northeastern states of Massachusetts, Pennsylvania, and New York. One, Samuel Omelveny, was born in Ireland.[15]

[13] *Dictionary of American Biography,* s.v. "Thomas, Jesse B."; Alvord, pp. 425, 430–32.
[14] Carpenter, pp. 335–36.
[15] Ibid., pp. 330–47. The question of replacement of delegates came up when one convention member died four days after the convention began. A committee appointed two days later to consider the election of a representative to take his place reported "that an election could not be effected in time to answer the purpose of giving the said county their full representation in this convention before the same will have risen," and their report was concurred in by the convention. *Journal of the Convention* (1818), pp. 366, 389.

CONVENTION PROCEEDINGS

During late July and early August of 1818 the elected delegates made their way to the old French town of Kaskaskia, located on a low, level stretch between the Kaskaskia and Mississippi rivers. The convention was called to order on the first Monday in August, with all delegates present but four.[16]

On the second day the delegates examined the results of the census to ascertain officially whether they were authorized to proceed with the framing of a constitution. On June 17, 1818, a statement published by the *Illinois Intelligencer* of all the census reports except that of Franklin County showed a population of 34,620. Obviously the territory was not going to attain the required forty thousand unless supplementary reports turned in during July showed a sharp increase. Miraculously, they did — the reports examined in the convention showed a population of 40,258, an increase of 5,638 over the first reports in June. The convention appears to have raised no question as to the accuracy of this census although later investigators were dubious about its results.[17] After the census report was accepted, "a committee of fifteen, one from each county, [was] appointed to frame and report to this convention a constitution. . . ."[18] The chairman of this committee was General Leonard White of Gallatin, but from contemporary accounts the guiding spirit was Elias Kent Kane.

The committee took only one week to draft the constitution, and the entire convention debated its provisions only two weeks before approving the constitution in final form on August 26. This haste was due not only to the desire to beat Missouri to statehood, but also to the fact that the Illinois constitution makers were typical of writ-

[16] *Journal of the Convention* (1818), pp. 355–57.
[17] Suspicion of the accuracy of the 1818 census is raised by a comparison with the U.S. census of 1820. The 1818 count for Gallatin County totalled 101 more than the U.S. census two years later, during which time the permanent population of the county was likely to have increased. Washington County attracted even more permanent settlers during these two years, and yet its 1818 census report showed 190 more residents than the 1820 U.S. census. Buck, *Illinois in 1818,* pp. 240, 264–65.
[18] *Journal of the Convention* (1818), pp. 359–60; Thomas Ford, *History of Illinois from Its Commencement as a State in 1818 to 1847* (Chicago: S. C. Griggs & Co., 1854), p. 24. Ford was governor of Illinois from 1843 to 1847.

ers of frontier constitutions in their impatience with the time and effort it would have taken to formulate a flexible, coherent statement of the principles of state government. Therefore the Illinois Constitution of 1818 was short and rudimentary. It borrowed provisions wholesale from other constitutions and made innovations only when called for by immediate needs and personalities. This method of constitution making probably reflected the sentiments of a majority of Illinois settlers at the time, but set a pattern of improvisation and expediency which was to lead to difficulties in the future.

For models the Illinois constitution makers had the federal Constitution and the state constitutions of the revolutionary period. Constitutions written for the frontier states of Tennessee and Kentucky in 1796 and 1799, for Ohio in 1802, and for Indiana in 1816 provided immediate examples for provisions in the Illinois Constitution. Wholesale borrowing can be seen in the preamble to the Illinois Constitution and in Article I dealing with the separation of power into three departments. Both sections strongly resemble the wording of corresponding provisions in the Indiana and Kentucky constitutions.[19]

Illinois also adopted the familiar pattern of a bicameral legislature. Both senators and representatives would be apportioned according to the number of white inhabitants. Representatives were to number not less than twenty-seven or more than thirty-six until the population reached one hundred thousand. Senators were to total at least one-third and never more than one-half the number of representatives. Each house was to be reapportioned according to census figures every five years. Representatives had to be at least twenty-one years of age and senators twenty-five and both had to be United States citizens and twelve-month residents of their districts. Illinois, like Indiana, had no specific property requirement for General Assembly members, but did stipulate that they pay a state or county tax. At first, section 2 of Article II provided for annual sessions of

[19] The 1818 constitution can be found in a number of sources, including Verlie, pp. 25–47, and the *Illinois Blue Book, 1917–18,* pp. 337–46. For comparisons with other state constitutions, see Francis Thorpe, *The Federal and State Constitutions,* 7 vols. (Washington, D.C.: U.S. Government Printing Office, 1909).

the legislature, but at a second reading the annual provision was changed to biennial.[20]

Illinois's territorial experience was the greatest influence in establishing suffrage requirements in the new constitution. The Ordinance of 1787 had restricted suffrage in new territories to free-holders, but in Illinois Territory, as in others in the Northwest, conflicting claims of Indian tribes, old French settlers, and land speculators made it almost impossible to secure titles to land, so that few could claim legal freehold status. Therefore, in 1812 Congress abandoned the freehold requirement and gave the vote to any adult male who had resided in the territory a year and had paid a state or county tax. The convention delegates continued this policy, also following the lead of Indiana and the earlier examples of New Hampshire, Georgia, Maryland, and South Carolina; suffrage was granted to "all white male inhabitants above the age of 21 years, having resided in the state six months next preceding the election." Excepted were those "convicted of bribery, perjury or any other infamous crime." By this provision, the vote was extended even to aliens, who had also been allowed to vote and to hold office in Illinois Territory. On the other hand, free blacks as well as women were denied suffrage. All votes were to be given viva voce, but this provision could be altered by the General Assembly.

Article III on the executive was copied largely from Ohio's constitution and reflected popular distaste for the broad powers wielded by colonial and territorial governors. The convention members saw the legislature, which had been popularly elected when Illinois was a territory, as the real expression of the people's will and therefore the rightful repository of power in the three-part government. Thus, the executive's powers were greatly restricted. Unlike some of the other state governors who were allowed to serve only two years, the

[20] Buck, *Illinois in 1818*, pp. 269, 271. Biennial meetings were proposed in the August 19 *Illinois Intelligencer* in a "letter from an inhabitant of St. Clair county, to a Member of the Convention." The writer contended that "the lapse of a few months will not furnish a sufficient test of the qualities of the theory or practicable operation of the laws passed at any one session," and criticized the territorial legislature, meeting annually, for "enacting at one session and repealing at the next, until our laws on some subjects have become so confused, that to use a common adage, 'a Philadelphia lawyer' could not tell what these acts mean, nor even how much of them is in force." Saving expenses was another reason for the change.

Illinois governor was granted a four-year term, but he was pro-hibited from succeeding himself. Neither limit nor specification was placed on remuneration to members of the General Assembly, but the governor's annual salary was limited to $1,000 until the year 1824, and that of his appointee, the secretary of state, to $600.

No exclusive veto power was granted to the governor, reflecting Illinois's dislike of the absolute veto exercised by territorial governors. Instead, the New York system of a council of revision was adopted, probably through the influence of New York native Elias Kent Kane. The council of revision consisted of the governor and the judges of the supreme court "or a major part of them together with the governor." Its function would be to "revise all bills about to be passed into laws" and to return those of which it disapproved, to-gether with its objections, to the house where they had originated. However, bills could be passed over the objections of the council of revision by a majority vote of the legislature.

In Article III, section 22, the governor was given an extensive appointing power; with the exception of a state treasurer and public printer to be elected biennially by the legislature, he was to appoint "all officers whose offices are established by this constitution, or shall be established by law, and whose appointments are not herein other-wise provided for." However, section 10 of the schedule, adopted after Article III, made this power ambiguous. The confusion, lead-ing to great difficulties in the future, is blamed by Governor Thomas Ford in his *History of Illinois* on the desire of the convention mem-bers to assure one of the state offices to a particular person. Expect-ing Shadrach Bond to be elected governor and believing that Bond would not appoint the convention's choice, Elijah C. Berry, to be the first auditor of public accounts, the convention declared in the schedule that "an auditor of public accounts, an attorney general, and *such other officers for the state as may be necessary,* may be ap-pointed by the general assembly . . ." (italics added). This part of the schedule greatly encroached upon the appointing power given to the governor in Article III and was the source of controversy in the years ahead. What were "officers for the state"? The legislature decided that almost every office was, and it appointed canal com-missioners and agents, fund commissioners, commissioners of the board of public works, bank directors, state's attorneys, and others, sometimes by election and sometimes by passing laws appointing them to office by name. Ford described the difficulties:

> Sometimes one legislature, feeling pleased with the governor, would give him some appointing power, which their successors would take away, if they happened to quarrel with him. This constant chang- ing and shifting of powers from one co-ordinate branch of govern- ment to another, ... was one of the worst features of the govern- ment. It led to innumerable intrigues and corruptions, and for a long time destroyed the harmony between the executive and legis- lative departments. And all this was caused by the Convention of 1818, in the attempt to get one man into an office of no very con- siderable importance.[21]

Although we shall never know the intent of the 1818 delegates in regard to Berry and his office, we can see in the conflicting ap- pointment provisions an illustration of a continual problem in the writing and execution of constitutional principles: who should be given the power to fill important state offices? Should the officers be appointed, and if so, by whom, the governor, the legislature? Or, should the appointive power be divided between them, to keep them in balance? During the 1830s this conflict was resolved in favor of neither the governor nor the legislature. The trend at this time was to fill important state offices by popular election.

A similar conflict arose over appointment of the judiciary. The constitution provided for a supreme court consisting of a chief justice and three associate justices, with appellate jurisdiction only, except in certain special cases. These justices were to be appointed by joint ballot of the two houses of the legislature, and their term was to end in 1824, at which time they were to be commissioned indefinitely "during good behavior." The legislature was also given power to establish inferior courts and to appoint justices of the peace and determine their tenure, powers, and duties. However, the provision that "justices of the peace, when so appointed, shall be commissioned by the governor," led to controversy in later years over the division of the appointment power between the two branches of state government.

The article on slavery underwent considerable change from the

[21] Ford, p. 27.

committee's draft, and became a source of controversy in the constitution's approval by the United States Congress. The original draft of the first section was copied from the Ohio Constitution and stated that "there shall be neither slavery nor involuntary servitude in this state, otherwise than for the punishment of crimes, whereof the party shall have been duly convicted. . . ." Indenture was permissible only on condition that it was freely and voluntarily undertaken and that the indentured party should be compensated. Negroes and mulattoes could not thereafter be indentured for longer than one year.[22]

On second reading the first sentence was changed to read, "Neither slavery nor involuntary servitude shall *hereafter* be introduced into this state. . . ." The phrasing concerning indentures, which under the Ohio Constitution read "under pretence of indenture or otherwise," was changed to "under any indenture *hereafter* made"[23] (italics added). In this way the current property rights in slaves and indentured servants in Illinois were upheld.

A second section was added to this article prohibiting the hiring in Illinois of persons "bound to labor in any other state," except for slaves to work in the salt mines in Gallatin County, and they for a period not longer than one year at a time. The intention to protect existing property rights and to permit slaves to work in the salt mines, a task believed to be physically impossible for white men, was made even stronger when, at the third reading of the article, another section was inserted to further insure the continuation of a supply of unfree labor in Illinois:

Each and every person who has been bound to service by contract or indenture, in virtue of the laws of Illinois territory, . . . without fraud or collusion, shall be held to a specific performance of their contracts or indentures; and such negroes, and mulattoes as have been registered in conformity with the aforesaid laws shall serve out the time appointed by said laws. . . .[24]

The children of slaves and indentured servants were to become free — males at the age of twenty-one and females at the age of eighteen.

[22] *Journal of the Convention* (1818), p. 380.
[23] Ibid., p. 400.
[24] Ibid., p. 411.

Illinois could conceivably be assured of some unfree labor until at least 1839.[25]

The compromise on the slavery article guaranteed both that Illinois would be a free state and that existing property rights would be protected. The slavery clauses passed by narrow margins, but no clearcut sectional or factional division among the members can be traced.[26]

The Illinois Constitution omitted a provision which had been included in the Ohio and Indiana constitutions expressly prohibiting amendment to allow the introduction of slavery. The suspicion that this omission was intentional is confirmed by the efforts of the proslavery group to call a constitutional convention in 1824.

The article on the amending process was copied from the Ohio Constitution. The Illinois Constitution could be amended only by the calling of a convention. Two-thirds of the General Assembly might recommend to the voters "to vote for or against a convention." One provision which was to hamper constitutional change for years required that if a majority "of all the citizens of the state voting for representatives" voted in the affirmative, the next legislature was to call such a convention. This meant that a voter's failure to express himself on a convention call would count as a vote against the call. The Illinois convention had before it another example which could have been used: the Indiana Constitution, following precedents established in Massachusetts in 1780 and New Hampshire in 1792, stipulated an automatic election on the question of calling a convention every twelve years. The election did not have to be initiated by the legislature.[27] Illinois borrowed extensively from the Indiana Constitution, but chose not to copy this provision.

Like all other early midwestern constitutions, the Illinois Constitution contained a bill of rights modeled on those of revolutionary state constitutions and the Constitution of the United States. The wording of the Illinois Bill of Rights was taken largely from the Ohio, Kentucky, Tennessee, and Indiana constitutions, with little

[25] The state of Illinois numbered 917 slaves in her 1820 population of 55,162, and 331 slaves in a total 1840 population of 476,183. U.S., Bureau of the Census, *Statistical View of the United States: ... A Compendium of the Seventh Census* (1850), p. 82.

[26] *Journal of the Convention* (1818), pp. 401, 411.

[27] Thorpe, 2:1057–59.

thought given to changes in these basic statements of individual rights. Additions unique to the Illinois Constitution were section 20, which concerned the equality of taxation and introduced the property tax as a means to that end, and section 21, which prohibited "any banks or monied institutions in this state, but those already provided for in the law." This may have been an attempt to prevent the establishment in Illinois of a branch of the Bank of the United States, whose image was that of a monopolistic creation of the moneyed East. On the other hand, a state bank was explicitly permitted, and was probably desired both by the public and by the convention delegates. This provision was to be the cause of many future problems.

A committee of five worked out a schedule to put the constitution in force. The schedule included such items as the apportionment of the two legislative houses for the first election of the General Assembly and the transfer of bonds and other financial contracts from territorial to state government. However, the schedule also contained some provisions which should have been included in the body of the constitution. For example, Article III stipulated that candidates for the position of lieutenant governor meet the same qualifications as candidates for governor, that is, age of thirty years, a thirty-year U.S. citizenship, and a two-year residence in the state. However, the convention wanted Colonel Pierre Menard, an old settler and a Frenchman, to be lieutenant governor. He had not been naturalized until a year or so before the convention, so in the schedule the thirty-year citizenship requirement was dropped.[28]

An issue of controversy second only to that concerning slavery was the location of the state capital. Despite the efforts of speculators who wanted to sell their own land to the government, others, who hoped the state itself might receive the profit from speculation by building the capital on unsurveyed, unregistered lands, won out.[29] The schedule directed the General Assembly to petition the federal government for land on the Kaskaskia River east of the third meridian. The convention's choice of a previously unsettled, inconvenient area met with disapproval from many quarters. The sched-

[28] Ford, p. 26.
[29] *Journal of the Convention* (1818), pp. 403, 423–24.

ule provided that the proposed site, later named Vandalia, should be the seat of government for twenty years. At the end of that time, there was another bitter fight over the capital's location and it was moved to Springfield.

The convention adjourned August 24, three weeks after deliberations began. Upon news of the completion of the writing of Illinois's constitution, the citizens of Kaskaskia held an informal celebration, as described in the *Illinois Intelligencer:*

> On this important occasion, the citizens of the town assembled to fire a federal salute to perpetuate the remembrance of the day when our constitution was signed and sealed. As many of the independent company of the town as were requisite to man the field piece, appeared at the capitol, in uniform, with their colours flying, (being the flag of the union as adopted by the last act of Congress,) accompanied by the principal field officers. Upon the signing of the constitution, and the convention being about to adjourn they were invited by the committee of arrangements to join in the feu de joie.

> The field piece was placed in front of the capitol, the military officers a few paces in its rear — the governor, secretary, delegate to congress, and most of the territorial officers, accompanying the members of the convention, took their positions a few paces in the rear: The salute was commenced — 20 rounds were fired, and one for the new state of Illinois, which was accompanied by the following pledge, from the independent corps: "Under these colours, we pledge ourselves to support the constitution of Illinois."

> This was truly a proud day for the citizens of Illinois — a day on which hung the prosperity and hopes of thousands yet to follow — a day which will long be remembered and spoken of with enthusiastic pride; as a day connected with the permanent prosperity of our literary, political and religious institutions — as the main pillar in the edifice of our state independence, and justly the basis of our future greatness.[30]

This festive occasion was the only evidence of public feeling towards the new constitution. Although some states were submitting their proposed constitutions to a popular vote, including Mississippi in

[30] *Illinois Intelligencer,* September 2, 1818.

1817 and Connecticut in 1818, no suggestion of such a procedure seems to have been made in Illinois.[31]

APPROVAL OF THE CONSTITUTION

The Illinois Constitution did require approval by Congress and the President of the United States, however. The debate in the House previewed the more publicized debate three months later over the admission of Missouri. Northeastern delegates viewed the admission of a new western state with suspicion, particularly since Illinois's large southern population indicated that in sectional disputes the proposed new state would align with the southern bloc. Representative Tallmadge of New York, who was later to lead the fight against the admission of Missouri as a slave state, demanded further evidence that Illinois had the requisite population and held that "the principle of slavery, if not adopted in the constitution, was at least not sufficiently prohibited." He recalled that the Ordinance of 1787 prohibited slavery in the entire Northwest Territory, while the sixth article of the Illinois Constitution "contravened this stipulation, either in the letter or the spirit." Tallmadge pointed approvingly to the strong prohibition of slavery found in the constitution of neighboring Indiana: he believed that Congress should insist that "slavery should be absolutely prohibited in all states erected within the Northwest Territory."[32]

Representatives Poindexter of Mississippi and Anderson of Kentucky answered Tallmadge by proclaiming the impracticability of regulating a state's constitution, for if after admission, a constitution was to be changed to admit slavery, there was nothing Congress could do about it. Anderson doubted whether Congress "had a right to proscribe any condition respecting slavery" in the territories — the doctrine of Calhoun twenty years later. Tallmadge disagreed, insisting that Congress did have the power to prevent slavery in the territories and protesting that a state could not change its constitution at will, on which point he was disputed by Congressman (and future President) William Henry Harrison of Ohio. Harrison, al-

[31] Buck, *Illinois in 1818,* p. 292.
[32] U.S., Congress, *Annals of Congress,* 15th Cong., 2d sess., 1818, 33, pt. 1: 305–11.

though he sincerely wished Illinois had emancipated its slaves or prohibited any future slavery as Indiana had, admitted that he had always considered the Northwest Ordinance a "dead letter."[33]

This ended the floor debate in the House, and the resolution to admit Illinois carried by a vote of 117 to 34. The vote was divided on sectional lines. Of the thirty-four voting against the resolution, thirty-three were from the North.[34]

The Senate passed the resolution without debate,[35] and when President Monroe signed it December 3, Illinois's new constitution went into effect.

THE SLAVERY CONVENTION

The slavery issue in Illinois was not settled by her admission as a free state. In fact, only five years after adoption of the 1818 constitution, attempts were made to change it. Many had suspected that the exclusion from the constitution of a prohibition against future slavery indicated the hopes of proslavery men in Illinois. These suspicions were confirmed in 1823 as attempts were made to call a convention for the purpose of changing the constitution to permit slavery in the state.

Proslavery sentiment in Illinois had increased with the financial crisis occurring after 1820; many felt slavery would attract prosperous planters who would spend money freely, buy up the land of disillusioned settlers who wanted to leave, and pay taxes. The example of Missouri, now admitted as a slave state and attracting wealthy slaveholding settlers, served as a strong influence, particularly in the southern counties of Illinois.

The slavery question had already been a decisive issue in the 1822 election for governor. At that time, Edward Coles, an antislavery man, had narrowly defeated Joseph B. Phillips, whose supporters frankly invited proslavery assistance. The victory for Coles came only because the opposition was split between Phillips and another candidate. After his election, Coles immediately pushed the slavery issue, calling for the abolition of such slavery as had been permitted

---

[33] Ibid., p. 311.
[34] U.S., Congress, House, *Journal*, 15th Cong., 2d sess., p. 30.
[35] U.S., Congress, Senate, *Journal*, 15th Cong., 2d sess., p. 43.

under the 1818 constitution, repeal of the black code,[36] and passage of laws against the kidnapping of free blacks. This provided a golden opportunity for the proslavery elements in the General Assembly. The Senate replied that the legislature presently had no power to abolish existing slavery, but that the whole question could be considered by a constitutional convention. By a vote of twelve to six, the Senate approved a call for a constitutional convention, with the intent of legalizing rather than abolishing slavery in Illinois.

The bill calling for a convention met stiffer opposition in the House, where the members were deeply divided on the question. On February 11, a vote on the issue carried 23 to 13, but did not receive the necessary two-thirds majority; one more vote was needed, and there was a way to get it. The election for one of the seats was contested, and the House had originally voted to seat Nicholas Hansen over his opponent, John Shaw. Now, two months later, the House overturned its original decision, unseated Hansen, and replaced him with Shaw. With Shaw's vote, the bill to call a convention passed 24 to 12.[37]

The convention call had to be approved by the voters, and the election followed a heated campaign. According to Governor Ford, the proconvention, proslavery forces used a variety of tactics to demonstrate that public opinion was overwhelmingly behind them. The night after passage of the resolution calling for a convention referendum, the convention party formed a procession. Led by three supreme court justices and the lieutenant governor, a majority of the legislature and a number of townspeople marched on the residences of Governor Coles and other political opponents.[38] The anticonvention forces quickly began to organize their opposition. The St. Clair County Society for the Prevention of Slavery in the State

[36] The first legislature of the state of Illinois had passed severe laws restricting the movement, immigration, and labor of free blacks, their rights to serve as witnesses in court, with stiff penalties against the harboring of fugitive slaves, as well as fines and punishments by whipping of disobedient slaves and servants. These laws, taken wholesale from constitutions of some of the southern states, were not enforced in Illinois, but were not taken off the statute books until 1865.

[37] Theodore C. Pease, *The Frontier State, 1818–1848,* vol. 2 of The Centennial History of Illinois (Springfield: Illinois Centennial Commission, 1918), pp. 78–80.

[38] Ford, p. 53.

of Illinois was founded March 22, 1823; in the next four months similar societies were founded in Monroe, Edwards, and Morgan counties. Antislavery caucuses were held to pick candidates for offices in the same election. Such church groups as the Friends of Humanity and the Christian Church Conference on the Wabash, as well as many Methodist circuit riders, assailed slavery and slaveholders. Governor Coles's friendship with Nicholas Biddle obtained for him connections with Philadelphia Quakers who supplied him with antislavery tracts which were distributed by the thousands, although their origin was not revealed.[39]

The proconvention organizers had behind them several newspapers — Henry Eddy's *Illinois Gazette,* the Kaskaskia *Republican Advocate,* and the *Illinois Republican* of Edwardsville. Many influential politicians in Illinois supported a convention. The convention backers did not name slavery as their reason for calling a convention, but letters and editorials show the drift of their arguments. Some claimed that slavery would be ended more quickly by its diffusion over as large an area as possible, and that the slaves themselves would benefit by exposure to humane Illinois treatment. Others pointed to the material advantage to the state of the settlement of wealthy planters, and the necessity of slavery for the continued prosperity of the Gallatin salt mines.

The antislavery forces replied to some of these charges, pointing out that diffusion of slavery had so far led to its expansion, not its demise. Further, the moral implications of slavery were examined, as in this passage from a letter to the *Illinois Intelligencer:*

> Is it not quite as unjust, because some men are black, to say there is a natural distinction as to them; and that black men, because they are black, ought to be slave. . . . is it not the hight [*sic*] of arrogance to allege that because we have strong feelings and cultivated minds it would be great cruelty to make slaves of us; but that because they are yet ignorant and uncultivated, it is no injury at all to them? Such a principle once admitted lays the foundation of a tyranny and injuce [*sic*] that have no end.[40]

[39] Elihu B. Washburne, *Sketch of Edward Coles, Second Governor of Illinois and of the Slavery Struggle of 1823–1824* (Chicago: Jansen, McClurg & Co., 1882), pp. 154–64.

[40] *Illinois Intelligencer,* May 21, 1824.

The immorality of slavery was stressed by Governor Coles, Congressman Daniel Pope Cook, Hooper Warren, editor of the *Edwardsville Spectator,* and David Blackwell, who was installed as editor of the *Illinois Intelligencer* after its purchase by Coles and a group of anti-conventionists. Powerful and important support also came from Morris Birkbeck, the English radical who, with George Flower, had established an English colony of settlers in Edwards County. Birkbeck had settled in Illinois because of the availability and cheapness of land and because of the state's exclusion of slavery, which he detested. Now, in an intense effort to prevent the establishment of slavery in Illinois, Birkbeck wrote letters to newspapers, signing them "Jonathan Freeman." He spoke in simple language to the small independent farmer, who, he argued, would be supplanted and degraded, not enriched, by opening Illinois to the slaveholding planter class.[41]

The debate over calling a convention lasted from the spring of 1823 until the general election on August 2, 1824, and Ford calls it a "long, excited, angry, bitter, and indignant contest."[42] The results of the election were definitive. Votes tallied 4,972 for a convention and 6,640 against it.

The vote showed a distinct sectional alignment, with southern counties supporting the convention and central counties opposing it, present-day northern Illinois not yet having been settled. Only two southern Illinois counties, Johnson and Union, did not give large majorities to calling a convention, whereas only one of the "northernmost" counties, Fayette, did not return a large majority against it. Pike, Fulton, Morgan, Sangamon, and Edgar all returned anti-convention majorities of better than 80 percent.[43] It was these coun-

[41] George Flower, *History of the English Settlement in Edwards County, Illinois, Founded in 1817 and 1818 by Morris Birkbeck and George Flower, Collections of the Chicago Historical Society* 1 (1882):227–45, 256.

[42] Ford, p. 54.

[43] Southern county voter percentages were as follows: In Gallatin 82 percent voted for a convention; in Pope, 69 percent; Alexander, 60 percent; Jackson, 66 percent; Hamilton, 67 percent; Jefferson, 70 percent; Wayne, 63 percent. Union, Johnson and White were close either way. North central counties were against a convention by fair majorities, and northern counties were overwhelmingly against it. In Pike County, the vote was 90 percent against a convention; in Fulton, 92 percent; Morgan, 91 percent; Sangamon, 83 percent; Clark, 79 percent; and Edgar, 99 percent. Theodore C. Pease, ed., *Illinois Election Returns, 1818–1848, Collections of the Illinois State Historical Library* 18 (Springfield, 1923):27–29.

ties which were becoming more populous, and whose settlers from Ohio and the Northeast were determined to keep Illinois free, which turned the tide against the convention.

The election in 1824 differs from the three other unsuccessful referenda calling for Illinois constitutional conventions. In 1824 a majority voted against the calling of a convention; other referenda failed because not enough of those voting at the elections cast either positive or negative votes on the convention question. The 1824 referendum was defeated on a specific issue on which the voters made themselves heard; the greatest cause of the failure of the other three was voter apathy. In 1824 the question of the admission of slavery into Illinois was settled, although the question of the place of blacks in the state was to come up more than once again in Illinois constitution making.

II

The Second Constitutional Convention

DEVELOPMENTS IN THE STATE, 1824–1842

The next attempt to call a constitutional convention in Illinois also failed, but under completely different circumstances. The opportunity to express themselves concerning the amendment or revision of the 1818 constitution was not offered to the voters again until 1842, and by that time the constitution was blamed for not having kept Illinois government functioning effectively and for the public benefit. The problems with the constitution seemed to lie, some felt, in the major changes in population which the state had undergone. Illinois, hard put to find forty thousand settlers to qualify for statehood in 1818, had a total population of 476,183 by 1840, an increase of over tenfold.[1]

Not only the population increase but the changing pattern of settlement was transforming Illinois. In the 1820s and 1830s Illinois settlers began to forsake the less productive agricultural lands between the Wabash and Mississippi rivers in the southern part of the state for the rich Sangamon River country. From the South and by way of the Erie Canal and the Great Lakes, new tides of population poured into the country north and west of the Illinois and Kaskaskia rivers. The early thirties saw the disappearance of the Indians from the prairies, with the Black Hawk War of 1832 marking their final retreat across the Mississippi. Farms were

[1] *Compendium of the Seventh Census,* p. 133.

carved out of the wilderness as tract after tract of government land was put up for sale at land offices at Galena, Chicago, Quincy, and Danville. Speculators thrived on the sale of lots in proposed towns, especially in Chicago, which grew rapidly year by year. In 1832, Chicago was a tiny market town with two stores and 150 inhabitants; four years later it had 120 stores and a population of eight thousand. By 1842 Chicago was the market for "about one-half the State of Illinois, a large portion of Indiana, and a very considerable part of Wisconsin."[2] In 1850 its population was almost thirty thousand.[3]

Although most of Illinois's population influx came from other parts of the United States, foreign immigration began to play an important part in the thirties when a large group of Germans settled in the Belleville area. Many Irish became farmers when their work on the Illinois-Michigan Canal was paid for in canal land, and English, Scots, and Scandinavian settlers began to arrive.[4]

As Illinois grew more complex economically and socially, its political complexion also changed. The Jacksonian Era, in Illinois as elsewhere in the West, gave rise to formal political parties.[5] Although party alignments owed much to sectional divisions and personal followings, some distinct differences in ideology, particularly on broad economic issues, could be delineated. Two parties dominated the scene, the Democrats, the more popular party in Illinois, and Whigs. The Democrats geared their appeals mainly to agrarian interests, and capitalized on a general dislike and distrust of national banking systems. Voters were drawn to the Whig party for a number of reasons, above all because of opposition to the Democrats. Whig spokesmen were less antagonistic to the national bank and felt business and agrarian interests could be served by an internal improvement system and a protective tariff.

The Whigs were never able to elect a governor or United States

---

[2] *Chicago American*, September 14, 1841, quoted by Judson F. Lee, "Transportation in the Development of Northern Illinois Previous to 1860," *Journal of the Illinois State Historical Society* 10 (1917–18):24.

[3] *Compendium of the Seventh Census*, p. 347.

[4] In 1850 there were approximately 38,000 first-generation Germans in Illinois, 28,000 Irish, 18,600 English, 4,600 Scots, and 3,500 Scandinavians. William V. Pooley, *Settlement in Illinois from 1830 to 1850*, reprinted from the *Bulletin of the University of Wisconsin*, History Series 1 (Madison, 1908):495–502.

[5] Pease, *The Frontier State*, pp. 136, 278.

senator, nor carry Illinois's electoral votes for their presidential candidates, but they perceived the desire of the people of Illinois for enlarged freedom for business expansion and had an influence within the legislature far greater than their success at the ballot box. Many Democrats, while opposed to national public works projects, were perfectly willing to join with Whigs in support of state improvement projects which they felt would provide economic opportunities for all. Also, many Democrats who on the campaign trail preached the wickedness of banks elsewhere promoted the establishment of banks chartered and regulated by the state, either for the economic welfare of the "little man" or for their own personal ambition. Therefore the state, with both Whig and Democratic support, engaged in several financial enterprises which ended in disaster, bringing public disapproval on the legislature and on the state constitution which had allowed the legislature such freedom. The constitution had permitted the establishment of state banks "regulated by the legislature," but banks created and administered by the legislature in 1821 and 1834 both failed, with resulting financial hardship and loss of credit for the state.

During the same period, the legislature also undertook an internal improvements scheme, but only one of its projects, the Illinois-Michigan Canal, was successful. A plan to build a great system of railroads, for which the legislature appropriated $10 million in 1837, was soon abandoned. The collapse of the banks and the demise of the internal improvement system left Illinois heavily in debt, with its financial credit seriously impaired. The debt seemed almost impossible to pay, and there was some talk of repudiation until Thomas Ford became governor in 1842 and made strenuous efforts to force Illinois to assume its responsibilities and save its credit.[6]

The state's fiscal woes were an important reason for calling a convention: a new constitution could prevent future financial disasters by curbing and restricting the legislature. Further, in accordance with the national trend toward popular control of government, a new constitution could change the basis on which state offices were filled from appointive to elective.

[6] Ibid., p. 57–69, 194–235, 316–26. For more on the development of parties in this era, see Richard P. McCormick, *The Second American Party System* (1966) and Lee Benson, *The Concept of Jacksonian Democracy* (1961).

Convention Calls, 1842 and 1846

By 1842 the movement for a convention to rewrite the 1818 constitution had gained momentum. The disastrous condition of government was seen by the state's leaders as due not to inexperience, public apathy, or determination by individuals to enrich themselves at the public's expense, but rather to defects in the constitution, which could be corrected by the writing of a new document. In the desire to rewrite their constitution, Illinois citizens had before them examples from other states which had amended or rewritten their fundamental charters. In the 1820s Georgia, North Carolina, and Maryland had called conventions which revised and rewrote original constitutions, curbing the powers of the legislature and enhancing those of the executive, broadening suffrage, and extending the number of officers to be popularly elected. Mississippi adopted a new constitution in 1832. New York was to follow this trend in constitutional revision in 1846, as were Michigan, Maryland, and Ohio in 1850 and 1851.[7] The Illinois legislature, therefore, was echoing a general dissatisfaction with the performance of state constitutions when in 1842 it voted to submit the question of calling a constitutional convention to the voters.

When the general election was held on August 1, 1842, those voting on the question of a convention call did approve it, but a majority of those voting for representatives to the next General Assembly was required to pass the constitutional question, and the number fell 4,203 votes short.[8] Historian Arthur Charles Cole blames this failure on indifference on the part of the electorate, brought on by the hesitation of political spokesmen of the day to

[7] Fletcher M. Green, *Constitutional Development in the South Atlantic States, 1776–1860* (Chapel Hill: University of North Carolina Press, 1930), pp. 170–251; see also, Thorpe.

[8] The official election returns list 37,476 votes for a convention, and 23,282 votes against it. There are two figures for the total vote cast for representatives, 83,359 and 67,396. This confusion seems to have arisen from the tallying methods used by county clerks, some of whom neglected to return the number of votes cast for representatives. Others did not return votes cast for the convention, or else arrived at their figure by subtracting votes for a convention from those cast for representatives. In any case, the state calculated the fate of the convention using the higher figure of votes cast for representatives. Pease, *Election Returns*, pp. 132–34.

place specific reasons and needs for a convention before the voters.[9]

After this call failed, newspaper editors, Whigs and Democrats alike, increasingly condemned the old constitution and urged its drastic modification. By the time the question was again submitted to the voters at the August 3, 1846, general election, the public had been informed as to the serious necessity for changes in their constitution. The question was now approved by the required majority of those voting for representatives, with 58,715 voting for a convention and 19,244 voting against it.[10]

ELECTION OF DELEGATES

Now that a constitutional convention had been approved by the voters, the Fifteenth General Assembly designated April 3, 1847, for the election of delegates to the convention. The delegates were to assemble on June 7 at Springfield, the state capital since 1839, and were to receive the same per diem pay, four dollars, as members of the General Assembly.[11] The 1818 constitution specified that the number of delegates was to equal the number of members of the General Assembly, a workable number of 42 when the First General Assembly was first apportioned. However, by 1847 the General Assembly totalled 162 members; therefore, 162 convention members were elected, the largest number of delegates to attend any of Illinois's constitutional conventions, and too unwieldy a body for effective work.[12]

[9] Arthur C. Cole, ed., *The Constitutional Debates of 1847, Collections of the Illinois State Historical Library* 14 (Springfield, 1919):xv. The 1847 convention did not allot money for printing the convention debates. Cole's record is taken from contemporary accounts of convention proceedings in the *Illinois State Register* and the *Sangamon Journal*.

[10] Despite the difficulties in compiling an accurate vote (see footnote 8), Pease calculates that 106,169½ votes were cast for representatives and 58,716 votes were cast for a convention, so that the question passed by a constitutional majority of 5,631 votes. Although the 1842 convention call failed to receive a constitutional majority of approval in 56 of 99 Illinois counties, the 1846 call was approved in 59 counties by a majority of those voting for General Assembly representatives. In only 14 counties did those voting against outnumber those voting for a convention. Pease, *Election Returns,* pp. 168–70.

[11] *Laws of Illinois,* 1847, p. 33.

[12] John Moses, *Illinois, Historical and Statistical* . . . , 2 vols. (Chicago: Fergus Printing Co., 1889), 2:554.

Both Democrat and Whig party members had campaigned for the calling of a convention, and both threw themselves into the campaign for the election of delegates. The Democrats promised to work for an antibank provision, popular election of state officials, including supreme court judges, an effective veto power for the governor, and "the infusion of pure democratic principles into the fundamental law." The Whigs capitalized on the popular demand for "economy and reform"; they hoped to exclude foreigners from voting and to prevent banking from being excluded. The Democrats, the majority party, emphasized party regularity in choosing delegates, but were weakened by a group of probank men within their ranks; the Whigs, as befitting the minority, claimed that the convention delegates should be chosen without regard to party affiliation.[13] The Whig strategy was successful in large part, as seventy-one Whigs were elected to ninety-one Democrats, still a minority but a large enough minority to prevent the making of a strictly partisan constitution.[14]

The makeup of the convention delegation reflected both the movement of population into Illinois and the continuing agrarian character of the state. Only 7 delegates were natives of Illinois; 26 were from New England, 38 from the Middle States, 35 from the South Atlantic seaboard, 41 from Kentucky and Tennessee, and 10 from Ohio and Indiana. As evidence of foreign immigration, 3 convention members were natives of Scotland, one was from Ireland, and 2 had been born in Germany. Farmers outnumbered lawyers 76 to 54.[15]

In 1848 as in 1818 membership in the convention marked the beginning or continuance of political careers for many delegates. In later years seven delegates were elected to the U.S. Congress, eight

[13] Cole, *Constitutional Debates of 1847*, p. xvi.

[14] Pease, *Election Returns*, pp. 437–63.

[15] The affinity of the farmer with the Democratic party is shown by a comparison of occupation with party affiliation. Forty-nine of the farmer-delegates were Democrats, while 28 were Whigs; 25 lawyers were Democrats, while 27 were Whigs. Farmers made up 54 percent of the Democratic delegation and 39 percent of the Whig delegation, while lawyers constituted 27 percent of the Democratic and 38 percent of the Whig delegations. Some caution must be used in delineating occupations in this way, however: to gain favor with the electorate some delegates termed themselves "farmers" when they were also teachers, merchants, or sawmill owners.

became members of the state legislature, and seven became circuit court judges. Five convention members were senators and six were representatives in the current General Assembly, including Newton Cloud, president of the convention and speaker of the House of Representatives from 1846 to 1848. John M. Palmer, a Democrat in 1847, helped found the Republican party in 1856, and served as governor of Illinois from 1869 to 1873, during the writing of another constitution. David Davis, eminent lawyer and friend of Abraham Lincoln, was appointed a U.S. circuit judge soon after his convention service, and served as a U.S. Supreme Court justice from 1862 to 1877, when he resigned to become senator from Illinois. Several delegates also served in later constitutional conventions — three in 1862, three in 1869–70, and one, John Dement, in 1848, 1862, and 1869–70.[16]

CONVENTION PROCEEDINGS

The convention assembled in the House of Representatives in Springfield on June 7, 1847, and the election of a permanent president gave an early indication of the future course of the convention. The majority Democratic party was disorganized and unable to agree on a candidate until the temporary chairman, an antibank Democrat, was finally nominated. Morgan County had elected a bipartisan delegation, two Democrats and two Whigs. This group united and was able to hold the balance of power between the minority Whigs and the split Democrats. With the help of Whigs and those Democrats who advocated a regulated banking system, Newton Cloud, a Morgan County Democrat, was elected. On the first ballot, Cloud received eighty-four votes and Casey sixty-five.[17] Thus the Whigs and "bank Democrats" combined for the first time in the convention, but not the last.

Henry W. Moore, a Gallatin County lawyer, was engaged to act as secretary and John A. Wilson as sergeant-at-arms of the convention; both were Democrats. Then, Sangamon County delegates, both Whigs, opposed the election of assistant secretaries and of an assis-

[16] Cole, *Constitutional Debates of 1847*, pp. 949–83.
[17] Cyrus Edwards, a Whig from Madison, and Archibald Williams, a Whig from Adams, received two votes each. Cole, *Constitutional Debates of 1847*, pp. 4, 949–83.

tant to the sergeant-at-arms, and proposed to ignore the legislative arrangement for the election of a printer with a fixed compensation and to let the work out to the lowest bidder. These proposals would fulfill the Whig pledge of "economy, retrenchment, and reform." The Democrats objected and claimed that matters pertaining to the number and pay of officers had been established in the legislative act which had ordered the convention; as the majority party, of course, they expected to fill the additional positions with party men.[18] After four days of debate, the Democrats won out, and the additional officers were elected. The four days' discussion, although initiated by partisan squabbling, did develop into a worthwhile consideration of the relative powers of the legislative authority of the state and of the convention. To what extent was the convention bound by the legislature's enabling act? This question, debated in 1847, was to come up again in conventions in 1862 and 1869, and was to be a factor in the defeat of the 1862 proposed constitution.

After the convention assigned committees to establish convention rules and work on various sections of the constitution,[19] the next weeks were taken up with meetings of these committees, plus the submission to the committees of various resolutions, many of which were debated on the floor. On three separate occasions, the convention was delayed by resolutions of sympathy for those killed in the Mexican War, or controversy over war protests. But despite factionalism and interruptions, the convention finished its work in less than three months, adjourning August 31.

CONSTITUTION OF 1848

The finished product of the 1847 convention was considerably longer and more detailed than that of 1818, both because of the increased complexity of the state's economy and government, and because the convention writers were attempting to exercise greater control over state government in the future than had been exercised in the past. It was not a party document. Democrats were unable

[18] Ibid., p. 47.

[19] Committees were appointed on the executive department, the judiciary, legislature, bill of rights, incorporations, revenue, elections and right of suffrage, finance, education, departments, counties, the militia, revision and amendment, miscellaneous subjects, and law reform. Ibid., pp. 65–66.

to achieve all their stated goals, as a coalition of Whigs and "bank Democrats" forced them to compromise on several key issues. This, although leaving many who believed in Democratic principles dissatisfied, helped insure the support of both parties for the passage of the constitution.

A major effort was made by the delegates to correct all mistakes made in the 1818 document. This was a praiseworthy goal, but it was often effected by inserting restrictive statutory material into the constitution. As a result, many provisions quickly became obsolete. The intent to correct old mistakes was evident in the preamble. When the 1818 constitution was written, a sect of Covenanters in Randolph County presented petitions asking that "this convention may declare the scriptures to be the word of God, and that the constitution is founded upon the same."[20] The petitions were ignored, and according to Governor Ford, the Covenanters for many years "refused to work the roads under the laws, serve on juries, hold any office, or do any other act showing that they recognized the government."[21] Remembering this, Judge Lockwood of Morgan County created an addition to the preamble, which stated that "We, the people of the State of Illinois [are] grateful to Almighty God, for the civil, political and religious liberty which He hath so long permitted us to enjoy, and looking to Him for a blessing upon our endeavors to secure and transmit the same unimpaired to succeeding generations."[22] Thus the 1847 constitution writers sought to keep from offending any religious group and wrote a provision in response to a specific problem from the past which was unlikely to reoccur.

The Illinois constitution makers echoed actions of other state constitutional revisers of the period in greatly limiting the power of the legislature, both because Jacksonian Democracy emphasized the executive as the embodiment of the best interests of the people, and because excesses of the General Assembly had almost bankrupted the state through the creation of banks and internal improvements. Both the ages and residence requirements for representatives and senators

[20] *Journal of the Convention* (1818), p. 365.
[21] Ford, p. 25.
[22] This addition to the preamble remained in constitutions written in 1862, 1869–70, 1920–22, and 1969–70.

were increased. The size of the General Assembly was decreased from 162 to 100 members, 75 representatives and 25 senators, specifically apportioned in section 40 of Article III. As the population grew, the number of representatives could be increased to as many as 100 and a new apportionment "according to the number of white inhabitants" was to be made every ten years, after the results of the federal census were known.[23]

As part of the convention's "economy drive" and attempts to curtail the legislature, the salaries of senators and representatives were fixed in the constitution at two dollars per day for the first forty-two days' attendance, and one dollar per day thereafter. These ridiculously low salaries, rigidly fixed in the constitution, had disastrous effects. Assembly members used subterfuges to get around the restrictions, or supplemented their pay with fees received for introducing hundreds of private bills, which became a major problem in the following decades. Private and unnecessary legislation was supposed to be discouraged by the measure reducing salaries after forty-two days, and by section 23, which stipulated that every bill had to be read on three different days in each house; however, the General Assembly took advantage of the clause which allowed three-fourths of the House to dispense with the latter rule "in case of urgency." Most bills were designated as "urgent."

Aware of the internal improvement debts still to be paid, the convention members made another attempt to prevent mistakes of the past. In section 37, the state was prohibited from contracting debts of over $50,000, and debts under this amount could be contracted only "to meet casual deficits or failures in revenues, . . . and the moneys thus borrowed shall be applied to the purpose for which they were obtained, or to repay the debt thus made, and to no other purpose. . . ." Debts "except for the purpose of repelling invasion, suppressing insurrection, or defending the state in war" had to be approved by the electorate at a general election. This provision greatly limited government flexibility; it was designed with past mistakes rather than future needs in mind.

---

[23] Illinois, *Constitution* (1848), Art. III, sec. 8. The 1848 constitution is found in various sources, including the *Journal of the Convention Assembled at Springfield, June 7, 1847* (Springfield, 1847), and Verlie, pp. 51–99. References here will be given by article and section only.

The state debt which already had been contracted, however, was not repudiated by the convention. A special provision, to be voted on separately, provided for the assessment of a two mill tax to be devoted exclusively to relieving this debt.

As the powers of the legislature were curtailed, those of the executive, though still rigidly circumscribed, were increased. The council of revision was abolished. It had served an advisory purpose from 1818 to 1848 by calling legislators' attention to technical defects in laws passed, but the supreme court ruling on the constitutionality of state laws was continually embarrassed by the fact that the justices had already passed on the laws in their role as members of the council of revision.[24] Also, the council's vetoes were seldom effective, as they could be overturned by a simple majority vote of the legislature. The Democrats, therefore, promised to give the governor an exclusive veto power which could be overturned only by two-thirds of the General Assembly. The governor obtained the veto in the new constitution, but the Whigs were able, with the help of some Democrats, to provide that his veto could be overruled by a simple majority of the members elected in each house. The governor's salary, like that of the legislators and the supreme court justices, was fixed in the constitution. A measure of his increased power is shown by the fact that his salary was raised from $1,000 to $1,500 per year, while that of the justices was raised to only $1,200. The secretary of state, auditor, and state treasurer were each to receive $800 per year. All of these salaries were unrealistic and inadequate during the next decades of financial growth.[25]

The ambiguities of the 1818 constitution, with its legislative appointment power inserted at the last minute, had led to confusion and conflict between the legislature and executive. In light of this unhappy experience and in accordance with an increased belief in popular participation in government, the Illinois and Wisconsin constitutions in 1848 established a general elective principle, soon to be copied by other states. The appointive power was taken away from both the legislature and the governor. All state and county officials were to be elected by the people. The new constitution also fixed

[24] Pease, *The Frontier State,* p. 34.
[25] Moses, 2:558.

terms of office for executive officers — four years for the secretary of state and the auditor, and a two-year term for the treasurer.[26]

Supreme court justices were also made elective in Article V of the 1848 constitution, after an unfortunate experience with legislative control of the courts. The 1818 constitution had given the General Assembly the power to increase the number of supreme court judges after 1824. The assembly could appoint judges, but could not remove them except through impeachment proceedings. Acting under this power, the legislature had drastically changed the composition of the court in 1841, when three of the four justices were Whigs, appointed before the Democrats came to power. Angered by an unfavorable supreme court decision, Democrats in the General Assembly passed a bill increasing the number of supreme court judges from four to nine. The bill was vetoed by the council of revision, but passed over the veto. Five new judges, all Democrats, were appointed, including Thomas Ford, Stephen A. Douglas, and 1847 convention member Walter B. Scates.[27]

To prevent the recurrence of such a situation, the new constitution permanently fixed the number of popularly-elected judges at three; this number could not be changed by the legislature. The justices were to serve nine-year terms. The Democrats, with their numerical superiority in the state, wanted to elect all three judges by the general ticket system, but again compromised with the Whigs, dividing the state into three sections, with one judge to be elected from each. As a concession to the Democrats, a provision was added allowing the General Assembly after the first election to change this arrangement to election by the whole state at large.

The 1848 constitution added unnecessary detail to Article V on courts. The 1818 constitution had merely given the General Assembly the power to create inferior courts, which the assembly had done

---

[26] A conflict over terms of office for the secretary of state had occurred in 1838. A. P. Field had been appointed secretary of state by Governor Edwards in 1826; he was still in office in 1838 when Democratic Governor Carlin attempted to remove him. Field, a Whig, stated that the constitution failed to specify the term for which the secretary of state was to be chosen, and he was upheld by the state Supreme Court, which ruled that while the term of office was not for life, the tenure, until the state should alter it, was dependent only on good behavior. Pease, *The Frontier State*, p. 278. See also Arnold Shankman, "Partisan Conflicts, 1839–1841, and the Illinois Constitution," *Journal of the Illinois State Historical Society* 63 (1970):337–67.

[27] Pease, *The Frontier State*, pp. 280 and 283.

by statute. The system had worked satisfactorily, so in 1848 the convention delegates incorporated the entire lower court system into the constitution, thereby restricting future legislatures from expanding and revising the court system to meet new needs.

Suffrage provoked a great deal of discussion, as it has in all Illinois's constitutional conventions. The Democrats, beneficiaries of most of the immigrant vote, wanted to retain the 1818 clause which gave the franchise to "all white male inhabitants above the age of 21 years"; the Whigs wanted to restrict this privilege to "all white male citizens." The Democrats accused the Whigs of "nativism," and defended the right of foreign residents to have a voice in elections; Whig spokesmen defended "true Americanism," and were able to gather enough Democratic defectors to place a citizenship qualification for voting in the new constitution. The vote was 81 to 60.[28]

Another amendment to the suffrage provision had little chance of approval, however. On June 22, Daniel Whitney, a Boone County doctor, moved to strike out the word "white" whenever it occurred in the resolutions regarding suffrage, but his motion favoring black suffrage lost, 137 to 8.[29]

All elections were now to be held by ballot only, ending a long dispute between advocates of the ballot and viva voce systems. The viva voce provision of the 1818 constitution had been changed to ballot in 1819, to viva voce in 1821, to ballot in 1823, and viva voce in 1829. The viva voce advocates felt that ballot voting implied some kind of clique or organization; ballot advocates protested that viva voce was easily used to intimidate voters. The viva voce system lost out as party organization formed and polling places multiplied, so that candidates could not appear at each location to ask for support.[30] A useful provision in Article VI established one biennial date, the Tuesday after the first Monday of November, for all general elections; until then as many as four general elections a year had been held.[31]

[28] *Journal of the Convention* (1847), pp. 206–207.

[29] The seven voting for the amendment were Whigs from far northern Illinois counties, all natives of New York and New England. *Journal of the Convention* (1847), p. 76.

[30] Pease, *The Frontier State*, p. 39.

[31] Moses, 2:554. This probably resulted from the establishment of the same date for presidential elections by Congress in 1845.

In recognition of the state's increased settlement and development, the constitution makers provided constitutional regulation for the public approval of establishment of new counties, and for the election of county sheriffs for two-year terms.[32] It was also necessary in 1847 to provide for township organization, a further indication of the changing origin of the settlers in Illinois. The county as the principal unit of rural government developed in the South, and was the only unit of local government in Illinois when the first constitution was written. By 1848 enough settlers were arriving from New England, where the town was the principal local governmental unit, that the General Assembly was directed to pass laws for township government within counties.[33]

Given the sad state of Illinois finances in 1847, revenue provisions were certain to take up a great deal of time in the convention. The revenue article repeated the 1818 provision for a property tax, but also included a section proposed by Whigs for a poll tax of "not less than fifty cents nor more than one dollar each," to be levied on "all able-bodied, free, white male inhabitants of this state," age twenty-one to sixty, who were eligible to vote. The reasons for the poll tax, as stated by Whig delegate James Davis, were to enable every class, and not just the property owner, to bear a share of the public burdens. Democrats replied that the poor already did their share in supporting the state through serving in the state militia and on jury duty, and in the road labor required of every man, which was valued at from two to five dollars per year. Nevertheless, with Democratic support from southern Illinois, the provision giving permission for the legislature to levy a poll tax carried.[34]

The convention's action on corporations highlights the schism in public thinking on this issue. On the one hand, legislative misdeeds and mistakes in regard to the establishment of corporations, as well as the popular image of the corporation as a sinister device to curb competition, led to the constitution's prohibiting the estab-

[32] Sheriffs could not serve more than one two-year term in any four-year period. Art. VII, sec. 7.

[33] In 1969 only seventeen counties were not under township organization, fourteen in the southernmost tip of the state, and the others south and west of Springfield. George D. Braden and Rubin G. Cohn, *The Illinois Constitution: An Annotated and Comparative Analysis* (Urbana: Institute of Government and Public Affairs, University of Illinois, 1969), p. 496.

[34] Cole, *Constitutional Debates of 1847,* pp. xxiv, 96.

lishment of corporations by special legislation. On the other hand, realization that the public desire for commercial and industrial development would necessitate the formation of more corporations, and that some of these, such as railroads, would have to be established by special acts, led to the insertion of a clause allowing special legislation "in cases where, in the judgment of the General Assembly, the objects of the corporation cannot be attained under general laws." In the next decades, the General Assembly decided time and time again that this clause applied, and passed bills allowing private corporations to be formed.

The major problem before the convention was the lack of sound theory with regard to banking. In different ways both Whigs and Democrats believed that the law must take responsibility for banking in order to provide a necessary framework for economic development, but the inherent power of a bank to affect economic conditions stirred fear and dislike. Some farmers looked on banking as a swindle because it made money out of selling time, and saw paper money as a suspicious device to undermine hard cash. Despite the fact that a majority of Democrats elected to the convention were against banks, resolutions "to prohibit the power of the Legislature to create or authorize any individuals, company or corporation, with banking powers in this State," and to "prohibit the circulation in this State of bank bills under the denomination of twenty dollars" were defeated 102 to 58.[35] Perhaps the example set by Wisconsin the year before was a factor, for Wisconsin's constitutional convention of 1846 had written a constitution which wholly prohibited banking and banned circulation of paper money of less than twenty-dollar denominations. This constitution was rejected by the voters.[36] Clearly most Illinois delegates in 1847 realized that Illinois could not get along without banks or paper money and that, despite rhetorical charges against the wickedness of banks, the public was aware of this also. The final compromise in the Illinois Constitution of 1848 prohibited state banks, but permitted the General Assembly to establish "corporations or associations with banking powers" only after approval by the voters at a general election.

[35] Ibid., pp. 101–103.
[36] Theodore A. Andersen, *A Century of Banking in Wisconsin* (Madison: State Historical Society of Wisconsin, 1954), pp. 14–21.

The 1847 convention gave little attention to the bill of rights, which was substantially unchanged from 1818. An addition was adopted to section 19 providing that "the legislature shall pass laws, with adequate penalties, preventing the intermarriage of whites with blacks, and no colored person shall ever, under any pretext, be allowed to hold any office of honor or profit in this state." However, Ninian Edwards pointed out to his fellow convention members that if the above rights could be taken away from blacks, it would imply that blacks were possessed of these rights in the first place as citizens of the United States. Since a majority of the delegates were unwilling to admit this, the provision was omitted from the final draft of the constitution.[37]

Party lines broke down in the debate over an article directing the General Assembly to pass laws to prohibit "free persons of color from immigrating to and settling in this state; and to effectually prevent owners of slaves from bringing them into this State for the purpose of setting them free." This proposal had been introduced by Benjamin Bond, a Whig from southern Illinois, and provoked debate and ill feeling between many of the delegates from northern and southern Illinois. Some members from northern Illinois believed that the provision was a "direct infringement of the constitution of the United States," while a southern Illinois delegate claimed that "our friends at the north do not understand our position at the south. They think us wrong because they cannot see the evils of this class of population among us." Another delegate doubted that blacks "were altogether human beings." A northern delegate protested that blacks had been degraded because of servitude and lack of education: "Take the heroes of Buena Vista and Cerro Gordo and carry them into a foreign land, and subject them to servitude, and the fourth generation will be as degraded as the negro race"; he felt blacks should be granted the "poor privilege of cultivating our soil and breathing our air."[38] The vote on the proposition, like the debate, was divided along sectional lines. The article prohibiting black immigration passed 87 to 56, to be submitted separately with the constitution. While some northern delegates did support it, only

[37] *Journal of the Convention* (1847), pp. 470, 475–76. The provision originally passed by a vote of 82 to 32.

[38] Cole, *Constitutional Debates of 1847,* pp. 201–38.

five negative votes came from delegates representing counties in southern Illinois.[39]

In considering an amendment process for the constitution, the Illinois delegates might have chosen periodic submission of the question of a convention call to the voters. New York's constitution of 1846 had followed the precedent of Massachusetts, New Hampshire, and Indiana in requiring the question of a new convention to be submitted to the voters at regular intervals, in New York's case every twenty years. In the 1850s Michigan, Maryland, Ohio, and Iowa were also to adopt this provision.[40] Periodic submission to the people of the convention question would appear to be consistent with the principle of increased popular participation in government embodied in the greater elective power established in the 1848 constitution; however, there is no evidence that it was seriously considered by Illinois constitution makers. Instead, two methods of amending the constitution were provided. A convention call could be initiated by the General Assembly and then approved in a general election by a majority of those voting for state representatives. This method was contained in the 1818 constitution. By the second method, amendments could be proposed in either branch of the General Assembly and approved by the electorate.

Some doubts were expressed in the convention as to the latter provision; Supreme Court Justice Walter B. Scates opposed giving the legislature the power to propose amendments to the constitution, as "they would never let it alone, but at every session would be tinkering at it." Other members, however, doubted that a provision for amending would mean numerous and extensive amendments, citing other state constitutions and the federal Constitution as examples.[41] They were certainly correct in this assumption, for in practice the difficulty of amending the constitution under the second section soon became apparent. The General Assembly was forbidden to propose amendments to more than one article of the constitution at the same session. Then, before submission to the electorate, an amendment had to be approved not only by two-thirds of all the

[39] *Journal of the Convention* (1847), pp. 155–56.
[40] See Thorpe; see also, Robert J. Martineau, "The Mandatory Referendum on Calling a State Constitutional Convention: Enforcing the People's Right to Reform Their Government," *Ohio State Law Journal* 31 (1970):421–55.
[41] Cole, *Constitutional Debates of 1847*, p. 200.

members elected in each house during one session, but also by a majority of the members of the *next* General Assembly. Then, the amendment would be submitted to the voters, where it could be put into effect by a majority of those voting for members of the House of Representatives at the same election. Under these difficult procedures the constitution was never amended.

The hurdle to constitutional amendment provided by Illinois delegates in 1847 illustrates a common contradiction in the purpose of state constitutions. On the one hand, the delegates inserted policy-making legislation into the constitution in the excessively detailed sections dealing with salaries and judicial reorganization. Yet, when faced with the possibility that their work might be amended or changed, they regarded their document as a broad, unchanging statement of fundamental principles, assuming that "wisdom would die with them and that nobody else should be permitted to disturb their labors, and interfere with what they had done."[42] Compared to changes in amending procedures in other states during the period, Illinois's 1848 provisions seem especially rigid. Explanations of this phenomenon might center on the many divisions within the state: Whigs versus Democrats, bank versus nonbank partisans, North versus South, old settlers versus new. These divisions increased suspicions on all sides that future tampering with the constitution, if made too easy, would be harmful. Therefore, the Illinois Constitution submitted to the voters in 1848 was a legislating document, but without the flexibility which might have made such a document effective.

The schedule for the constitution provided for its submission to the voters on the first Monday in March 1848, six months after the work of the convention was concluded. The constitution was submitted as a whole, except for articles on black immigration and on the levying of the two mill tax with which to pay the current state debt. These articles were submitted separately, and a sample poll book was included in the schedule so that there would be no misunderstanding.

[42] *Debates and Proceedings of the Constitutional Convention of the State of Illinois Convened at the City of Springfield, Tuesday, December 13, 1869,* 2 vols. (Springfield, 1870), 2:1316.

Approval of the Constitution

The important factor in the overwhelming approval of the constitution by the voters in March was probably the lack of strong opposition from any one group. Historian Theodore Pease estimated that only six newspapers in the state, some judges who would lose their jobs, and some "small fry politicians" opposed the constitution.[43] Germans, led by Gustave Koerner, opposed the citizenship requirement for suffrage but their opposition was mild because of their approval of other reforms.[44] Both political parties supported approval of the constitution, but without enthusiasm. It contained many compromises, and each side was jealous of the victories gained by the other. Yet, each was afraid to raise the cry of "party constitution" for fear that party bickering would alienate the support necessary for its approval. The completed constitution was signed and approved by 131 delegates; 7, all Democrats, refused to sign it, and 24 were absent.[45]

Democrats were unhappy because the Whigs, with some help, had carried almost every point they cared to dispute. One prominent Democrat called the constitution "a mongrel affair" likely to "make trouble." The *Chicago Democrat* correspondent complained that "the convention is too horribly *conservative* to be of much use. Liberal principles stand no chance whatever. . . ."[46] However, few Democrats were willing to provoke open hostility to the constitution; many of its provisions were decided improvements over the old provisions, and to the average voter the strict regard for economy displayed by the convention was attractive.[47]

Newspaper support was more enthusiastic than party support. Newspapers across Illinois kept interest alive in the constitution issue from the time the convention ended until the referendum in March six months later. The *Aurora Beacon* of February 10, 1848, probably expressed the general sentiment in saying that "the new consti-

[43] Pease, *The Frontier State*, p. 408.
[44] Gustave Koerner, *Memoirs of Gustave Koerner, 1809–1896*, 2 vols. (Cedar Rapids, Ia.: The Torch Press, 1909), 1:523–24.
[45] Cole, *Constitutional Debates of 1847*, p. 944.
[46] Ibid., p. xxix.
[47] The convention was so parsimonious that the members would not even approve expenditures for official reporting and printing of their debates. Cole, *Constitutional Debates of 1847*, pp. 72–81.

tution is not perfect, for it is the work of fallible men. Critics and hypercritics, many good men, and some who might be suspected of sinister motives, may condemn it; but it is, on the whole, a good Constitution — a republican one — and an immense improvement upon the old instrument."[48]

On March 6, 1848, the constitution and separate articles were submitted to the voters. The vote was light, but the constitution was approved by a majority of almost four to one, 60,585 favoring it and 15,903 opposed. Party divisions were not clearly drawn: the only county to register a negative vote, Monroe, was Democratic, but voters in Lawrence County, also Democratic, cast over 97 percent of their ballots for the constitution, as did Wabash and Mercer county voters, strongly Whig. Cook County approved the constitution by a margin of 53 to 47 percent.[49] Article XIV prohibiting black immigration was also approved by a large majority, 50,261 to 21,297. Most voters in the state, no matter where they lived, approved this article. Although they were opposed to slavery they did not want blacks in Illinois: blacks were discouraged from immigrating and could not serve in the militia, pay the poll tax, or vote. Article XV, which levied a tax on property to pay the state debt, received the smallest majority, 41,349 to 30,945, but also passed, with 57 percent voting to accept the tax burden.[50] The constitution went into effect on April 1, 1848.

[48] Pease, *The Frontier State,* p. 409.
[49] Pease, *Election Returns,* pp. 173–75.
[50] Ibid., pp. 176–81.

III

The Wartime Convention

CONVENTION REFERENDUMS, 1856 AND 1860

In 1856, only nine years after the last constitutional convention in Illinois, a referendum to call another was sent to the voters. The excessive restrictions written into the 1848 constitution and its inflexibility hampered state government. The amendment procedure was so difficult that the convention process seemed to be the only possible way to effect constitutional change.

Illinois newspapers made little mention of the convention question either before or after the election in 1856. That year political attention centered on the bitter state and national elections, where a major party realignment was taking place. In May of 1856, the Republican party had been formed in Illinois, bringing together Free Soilers, old-line Whigs, and many Democrats. In the November elections the new party showed its strength, winning all the major state offices and electing four of the eight United States congressmen. John C. Fremont, the Republican presidential candidate, lost the state to James Buchanan by only a narrow margin. Republican strength followed sectional lines: counties from Henry northeast to DuPage and Lake went strongly Republican, while southern counties between the Mississippi and the Wabash with few exceptions voted firmly Democratic. Convention call votes also divided sectionally, with many northern counties voting overwhelmingly for a call and many southern counties registering less than 100 votes in favor of it. But only a few of the voters — less than a third of the number who voted for governor — expressed themselves on the convention issue, and the call was decisively defeated.[1]

Four years later the presidential election focused even more attention on national party struggles, for two of the major contenders — Abraham Lincoln and Stephen A. Douglas — claimed Illinois as a political base.[2] Newspapers which in 1856 had hardly mentioned the convention call gave more attention to this one. The day before the election the *Illinois State Journal* carried a special notice urging approval of the call and warning voters that since the 1848 constitution required passage of a majority of those voting for representatives, a failure to vote would count as a negative vote.[3] After the election the legislature passed an enabling bill which provided for the election of delegates from the same districts and by the same procedures as state representatives. There were to be the same number of delegates as representatives, seventy-five at that time, and they would be compensated at the rate of four dollars per day. They would be elected November 5, 1861, and would convene January 7, 1862.[4]

THE PARTISAN DELEGATION

The campaign for delegates was quiet and the total vote was only about half that of the 1860 general election, but the results were a reversal for the Republican party. Though the Republicans in 1860 swept the state elections as they had in 1856, and carried the state for Abraham Lincoln as well, in 1861 only twenty-one Republicans as against forty-five regular Democrats were elected as delegates to the constitutional convention.[5]

This reversal may have occurred because of Republican apathy. The Civil War had just begun, and interest, particularly Republican

[1] Official Election Returns, November 4, 1856, State Archives, Springfield, Ill.; *Chicago Times,* November 13, 20, 1856.
[2] The official vote was 179,668 to 83,572. A total of forty-five counties cast majority votes against the call; thirty-nine of these were in southern Illinois. Official Election Returns, November 6, 1860, State Archives, Springfield, Ill. Transcripts of these returns are in the Illinois Historical Survey, Urbana.
[3] *Illinois State Journal,* November 5, 1860. The *Journal's* support of a convention was based on the hope that a new constitution could eliminate the two mill tax levied by the 1848 document to pay heavy state debts.
[4] *Laws of Illinois,* 1861, pp. 84–87.
[5] Seven other delegates were Fusionists or Union Democrats and the political affiliation of two others is doubtful. Moses, 2:655.

interest, did not center on a new state constitutional convention. Many Republican newspapers allowed delegate elections to pass with slight notice and little partisan appeal. However, the Republican defeat might have resulted from a genuine effort to make the convention nonpartisan. The *Illinois State Journal* later claimed that in 1861 Republicans had entered into agreements "that the convention should be nonpartisan in character and that the Democrats . . . should be liberally represented." The *Urbana Democrat* commented that "after years of most intense political excitement, it seems strange to see old party lines entirely blotted out and the people casting about, making choice of the best and most deserving without respect to former political organization." One historian credited the election of a Democratic majority to the simple fact that most of the prominent lawyers in the state were Democrats.[6]

However, the election of a Democratic majority to the constitutional convention could also be interpreted as a vindication of Democratic policies. Many of the state's problems at that time involved banks, corporations, and railroads. The Democratic party was the traditional enemy of these powers and a friend of the farmer, who was still the majority voter in Illinois. If the delegate vote was a genuine expression of Democratic sympathies, it was a faithful forecast of the coming election of a Democratic General Assembly in 1862, an election usually attributed to disillusion with Republicans because of early Union defeats in the war, corruption in the war department, and arbitrary arrests by federal authorities for "sedition."[7] In any case, the Democratic delegates believed they had received a mandate from the people to write a constitution based on Democratic principles.

CONVENTION PROCEEDINGS

On January 7, 1862, the delegates assembled in the capitol building in Springfield. Partisanship immediately became apparent in the

[6] *Illinois State Journal,* October 13, 1869; Oliver M. Dickerson, *The Illinois Constitutional Convention of 1862,* University of Illinois Studies in the Social Sciences, vol. 1, no. 9 (Urbana, 1905), pp. 7–8.
[7] See, for example, Theodore C. Pease, *The Story of Illinois,* 3d ed. rev. by Marguerite Jenison Pease (Chicago: University of Chicago Press, 1965), p. 170.

organization of the convention. The night before, the Democrats held a caucus and selected the officers for the convention who were duly elected the following day. All of these men were from the southern part of the state.

Convention proceedings soon aroused fears that the delegates were exceeding their legal powers. In 1862 this was a profound cause for concern, since many southern states had recently called conventions in which new constitutions were written repudiating the authority of the federal government. Now the Illinois delegates decided they could not take the oath for convention members prescribed by the legislature's enabling act. It required that they promise "to support the constitution of the United States and of this state," but they felt it inconsistent to swear to support the very constitution they were assembled to change. Therefore, the majority decided to take an oath to "support the constitution of the United States, and faithfully discharge the duties of [their] office as delegates of this convention, for the purpose of revising and amending the constitution of the state of Illinois."[8] This decision aroused some apprehension, especially among Republican newspapers such as the *Chicago Tribune* and *Illinois State Journal,* which expressed the opinion that the convention itself was not legal because the members had refused to take the prescribed oath.[9]

If the oath controversy had worried some observers, the next day's action was even more disturbing. Although the enabling act provided for a printer, a committee was appointed to determine whether the convention had the power to appoint its own printer. The majority report of the committee stated that the convention had full power to contract for its printing, and "that after due organization of the Convention, the law calling it is no longer binding; and that the Convention has supreme power in regard to all matters incident to the alteration and amendment of the constitution. . . ." In its exploration of the authority of the constitutional convention, the report went even further, stating that it considered the convention to be limited in power only by the federal Constitution, and not in

[8] *Journal of the Constitutional Convention of the State of Illinois Convened at Springfield, January 7, 1862* (Springfield, 1862), p. 3.
[9] Dickerson, pp. 10, 11.

any way by the state. This report was adopted by the convention by a vote of 55 to 14.[10]

Public unease over this interpretation of the convention's power eventually contributed to charges of disloyalty against convention delegates. Certainly the delegates did assume many powers over which their authority was debatable. Congress had proposed to amend the U.S. Constitution to prevent any further exclusion of slavery in the nation, and had provided specifically that the amendment be ratified by the state legislature rather than conventions. Nevertheless, the constitutional convention assumed the power to ratify this amendment and approved it on February 8.[11]

The convention became involved in other extraneous matters. Illinois had been allotted an additional seat in the House of Representatives, and the convention reapportioned the state into seven Republican and seven Democratic districts, pending approval by the voters. Then, despite the fact that it had no authority to do so, the convention adopted an ordinance appropriating $500,000 in 10 percent bonds for the relief of sick and wounded soldiers.[12] State officials refused to issue the bonds, and the whole plan came to nothing.

Soon after assembling in January, the convention began an investigation of the administration of the Republican Governor Richard Yates, asking him to furnish the convention with the amount and description of all indebtedness of the state, the names and salaries of all persons appointed by him to office since the war began, all

[10] *Journal of the Convention* (1862), pp. 19–22. Constitutional theorists have vigorously debated this concept of a constitutional convention: is it an embodiment of absolute popular sovereignty limited only by the federal constitution, or has it lost these extreme powers through effective political and institutional limitations? See Walter F. Dodd, *Revision and Amendment of State Constitutions* (Baltimore: The Johns Hopkins Press, 1910) and Roger S. Hoar, *Constitutional Conventions, Their Nature, Powers, and Limitations* (Boston: Little, Brown and Co., 1917) for support of the first theory, and John A. Jameson, *A Treatise on Constitutional Conventions: Their History, Powers, and Modes of Proceeding,* 4th ed. rev. (Chicago: Callaghan and Co., 1887), for support of the second interpretation. Some of the early criticism of the first interpretation by the 1862 delegates was muted by the adoption of a resolution on the same day providing that all changes in the constitution were to be submitted to a vote of the people.

[11] *Journal of the Convention* (1862), p. 358. The next legislature ratified this amendment as prescribed by Congress. Three states — Illinois, Ohio, and Maryland — approved this amendment, a compromise attempt to end the war.

[12] *Journal of the Convention* (1862), pp. 479, 1098–99.

contractors who had been or were to be paid out of the treasury, a copy of all contracts, and a list of quartermasters and other officers from the federal government, "plus all correspondence on this subject."[13] Clearly this was a Democratic attempt to embarrass the governor; Governor Yates on his part suspected the convention of disloyalty, as he said in a letter to Lyman Trumbull:

> Secession is deeper and stronger here [in the convention] than you have any idea — its advocates are numerous and powerful, and respectable. . . . I believe the leaders [of the convention] intend to disarm the State Government if they can — They would like civil war in Illinois. . . .[14]

The convention also investigated a widely-held belief that the Illinois military was being inadequately supplied, but the committee report affirmed that, despite "prejudiced rumors and speculations that floated over the country and filled the atmosphere around the capitol," the soldiers were indeed well provided for.[15]

In this divisive and partisan atmosphere the convention adjourned on March 24, 1862, its finished constitution signed by only fifty-four of the seventy-five original delegates. Of the Republicans, only the three Chicago members were willing to sign the document.[16]

PROPOSED CONSTITUTION OF 1862

The 1862 convention delegates attempted to eliminate many of the objectionable restrictions in the 1848 document, including the salary limitations for state officers. They also wrote new provisions for the enactment of homestead laws and for the establishment of free state schools.[17] The proposed constitution strengthened the executive branch by requiring a two-thirds vote in each house to overrule the governor's veto, and curbed the legislature by new restrictions on the passage of private bills, particularly those concerning corpo-

[13] Ibid., pp. 121–22.
[14] Letter from Richard Yates to Lyman Trumbull, February 14, 1862. Lyman Trumbull Papers, Illinois Historical Survey, Urbana.
[15] *Journal of the Convention* (1862), pp. 833–35.
[16] Ibid., pp. 1114–15.
[17] Constitution of 1862, Art. X, sec. 3; Art. V, sec. 14, 17. The proposed 1862 constitution can be found in the *Journal of the Convention* (1862) and other sources.

rations. During the 1850s the General Assembly had created scores of corporations. The "escape clause" in the 1848 constitution permitted passage of these private bills when, "in the judgment of the General Assembly, the objects of the corporation cannot be attained under general laws." This practice was completely prohibited in the proposed constitution.

The status of railroads in Illinois was the focus of a great deal of attention in the 1862 convention. Railroads had expanded in Illinois in the 1850s: the Illinois Central built and acquired a Y connecting Galena, Chicago, and Cairo, and between 1849 and 1856 other railroads built lines. Despite the welcoming of the railroads by Illinois residents and the eagerness of each town to have its own connecting line, railroads had aroused hostility by the 1860s through their high rates and the practice of rate discrimination. The Illinois Central was particularly criticized for these transgressions, and was further suspected of attempting to evade the required payments to the state for its charter privileges.[18] Demands were made upon the 1862 convention for state control of railroad rates and services, but resolutions to this effect were not adopted.[19] However, a provision holding the Illinois Central to its obligations to the state and another forbidding towns to mortgage themselves to finance the building of railroads were inserted into the proposed document.

The 1862 delegates wrote a banking and currency article controversial enough to be submitted separately to the voters. Antibank forces in the state, and particularly in the Democratic party, had been strengthened by events after 1847. A clause in the 1848 constitution had provided that a system of state-chartered banking could be created if approved by a popular vote. In 1851 the legislature over the governor's veto submitted a banking law to the people who approved it.[20] However, several of the banks established under this

[18] Arthur C. Cole, *The Era of the Civil War, 1848–1870*, vol. 3 of The Centennial History of Illinois (Chicago: Illinois Centennial Commission, 1922), p. 40–52; *Illinois State Register*, January 7, 1862; *Jonesboro Gazette*, February 12, 1859.

[19] One such resolution is found in the *Journal of the Convention* (1862), p. 148.

[20] The vote in favor of a banking system carried 37,650 to 31,413; with some exceptions, counties south of Springfield voted against the banking bill, and counties to the north voted in its favor. Official Election Returns, November 24, 1851, State Archives, Springfield.

system failed in the panics of 1854 and 1857,[21] and a great number of those remaining were ruined in 1861 when the secession of the southern states depreciated the value of the bank bonds to fifty or sixty cents on the dollar. Now the antibank forces in the convention pushed through a measure which prohibited the creation of any banking corporation or association in the state and virtually abrogated the charters of those banks existing at that time. No checks or any other written instruments could be circulated as money in place of specie. Even Democrats outside the convention criticized the banking provisions as unrealistic for a time when increased commerce made some form of banking and paper money essential.

Other provisions of the proposed constitution were more frankly partisan. The suffrage article allowed aliens to vote after a year's residence in Illinois because recent immigrants were expected to vote Democratic. Another provision was intended to reduce from four to two years the term of office for the governor and other state officers, and to call an election for new state officers in 1862, after Governor Yates and other Republicans had served only half their terms. Moreover, the Democrats reapportioned the state's legislative districts to their own advantage. Three years earlier a Democratic legislature had tried to do this, but Republican Governor William Bissell had vetoed the bill. Then in 1861 a Republican General Assembly had redistricted the state on Republican lines. Now, the Democrats at the constitutional convention attempted to do the same thing, and their apportionment of the state legislature was admittedly gerrymandered to favor their party.[22]

A final partisan effort, particularly strong since the Democrats at the convention were controlled by members from the southern part of the state, was made to enact clauses regarding the position of blacks in Illinois. Again, the introduction of this subject brought about sectional as well as party strife: northern delegates considered additional legislation regarding blacks in the state as unnecessary and likely to arouse more bitterness, while southern delegates insisted that their problems with blacks were not understood by the rest of the state.[23] Finally, three clauses were adopted, to be submitted

[21] Cole, *Era of the Civil War*, pp. 97–100.
[22] Dickerson, pp. 16–17, 43, 46, 47.
[23] Ibid., p. 13.

separately at the time of voting for the constitution. The first stated that "no negro or mulatto shall migrate to or settle in this state, after the adoption of this constitution." The second section prevented blacks from voting or holding office in the state, and the third instructed the General Assembly to pass all laws necessary to implement the other two provisions.[24]

THE CONSTITUTION REJECTED

The proposed constitution of 1862, written to uphold Democratic party principles and maintain the power of the party without compromise with the majority Republicans, alienated the many Republican newspapers in the state. By seizing on two main issues, the purported disloyalty of some convention members and the high taxes that could be levied under the new document, the Republican papers campaigned effectively against adoption of the proposed constitution.

During the convention sessions, the Republican papers had criticized members for their refusal to take the oath of allegiance to the 1848 constitution and for their assumption of extraconstitutional powers including the investigations of Governor Yates. However, the tumult and hysteria of the Civil War era gave them their most serious charge against the convention — the charge of disloyalty. By the end of the first week of convention meetings, the *Chicago Tribune* warned that "the people of Illinois will do well to watch the operations of a body known to comprise many actual sympathizers with the rebellion, rank secessionists at heart, who would be pleased to carry with them all Egypt into the Southern Confederacy." Charges were made that "a majority of the members of the Convention were members of the Knights of the Golden Circle," a prosecessionist group. These charges were considered serious enough to be investigated by the convention, whose committee found no substance whatsoever to the claim. Nevertheless, the newspapers, especially the *Chicago Tribune* and the *Illinois State Journal,* continued to raise the disloyalty issue. A vote for the constitution

[24] The delegate vote on the immigration clause was much closer than that on the suffrage clause. Section 1 passed 39 to 25; section 2 by 57 to 7. The delegates were overwhelmingly opposed to black suffrage. *Journal of the Convention* (1862), pp. 691–93, 1098.

was, they warned, not only a vote against the Republican party, but a vote against the national government and the war. The clauses on blacks and on apportionment, as well as the alleged increases in government costs, were also attacked.[25]

Democratic newspapers vigorously defended the constitution for its homestead provisions, Illinois Central Railroad clause, and elimination of defects in the 1848 document. The Democrats pointed to the repeal of the two mill tax, while the Republicans claimed that the constitution would raise taxes perhaps as much as $213,000 per year. The tax issue seemed to be the most widely discussed; out of fourteen exchanges on the merits of the constitution reprinted by the *Chicago Journal,* one half used the tax issue as their main argument.[26]

However, the loyalty issue in the midst of civil war was probably the most important factor in the constitution's defeat, and the Republican papers were accused of raising this issue purely for partisan purposes. The Democratic *Chicago Times* described their actions bitterly the day following the election:

> The majority of the convention were denounced as a band of secession conspirators, and the constitution has never been alluded to by a republican newspaper in any more gracious terms than a "secession ordinance," an "Egyptian swindle," or an "accursed thing," and no known supporter of it has escaped the epithets of "secessionist" and "traitor." And the result of the election, . . . according to these republican newspapers, was to decide whether Illinois is a loyal or a secession State.[27]

This adamant opposition to the constitution was more than enough to insure its defeat and on June 17, 1862, it went down by a vote of 141,103 to 125,052. The articles on banking and currency and congressional apportionment were also defeated, by narrower margins.[28]

The clauses on blacks were approved, although they did not take effect because of the defeat of the constitution. The clause prevent-

---

[25] Republican papers of May and June 1862, as quoted in Dickerson, pp. 21, 22, 48, 50, 51.

[26] Ibid., pp. 21, 22.

[27] *Chicago Times,* June 18, 1862.

[28] The vote on banking was 126,538 for and 130,339 against; on apportionment the vote was 125,732 for, 132,339 against. Official Election Returns, June 17, 1862, State Archives, Springfield.

ing black immigration was approved by a margin of two and one-half to one; the clause forbidding suffrage and officeholding by blacks, by a margin of almost six to one.[29] Although northern counties brought in majorities against the constitution and southern counties produced majorities approving it, the vote on the black propositions was overwhelmingly favorable statewide. Only five counties voted against all three sections of the article on blacks, and only six counties voted against the proposition that "no negro or mulatto shall have the right of suffrage, or hold any office in this state." In the midst of the Civil War, and only eight years before the ratification of the Fifteenth Amendment to the United States Constitution, the voters of the state were unwilling to give blacks the rights of citizenship in Illinois.

[29] The first section carried by 178,956 to 71,306; the second, 211,920 to 35,649; the third, 198,938 to 44,414. Ibid.

IV

The Fourth Constitutional Convention

CONVENTION CALL

After the Civil War was over and Reconstruction began, agitation resumed in Illinois for changes in the 1848 constitution. The legislature's position had become increasingly troublesome. On the one hand, the public had shown its disapproval of past misdeeds by constitutionally restricting the legislators' salaries and activities; on the other hand, the public still desired to extract personal benefit from the legislature whenever it liked. Therefore, the legislature was flooded with requests for private bills — to charter corporations and banks, to incorporate towns and villages, to grant divorces, to remit fines, to regulate the rate of interest on money. By the late 1860s the flood of private bills had dwarfed the number of public bills.[1] It was impossible for the legislators to know what each law concerned when hundreds were passed at every session. The sponsors of the bills augmented their constitutionally-restricted salaries with fees collected for the courtesy of introducing these private bills and working for their passage. The result was a serious abdication of responsibility to the general public in favor of private interests.

Salary limitations imposed on state officials for the sake of economy in 1848 were circumvented by various subterfuges. The legislature usually voted the governor "expense money" in an amount

[1] The legislative session of 1867 passed 1,071 private and only 202 public laws; the 1869 session passed 1,188 private and 385 public laws. *Laws of Illinois,* 1867, 1869. In these years the private and public laws were bound separately.

great enough to adequately supplement the $1,500 salary he was allowed under the constitution. Judges were paid additional sums for minor "services rendered," or their clerks were granted large salaries, part of which was kicked back to the judges.[2] Such methods of ignoring the letter of the constitution added little to the moral climate of the state government in Springfield.

The necessity for constitutional change was also rooted in the continuing growth of the state in population and in economic complexity. Despite the turmoil of war, the state's population increased by about 50 percent between 1860 and 1870. The most dramatic increase occurred in Chicago, which nearly tripled in size during the decade, with the foreign-born constituting nearly half of its population.[3] State government was proving incapable of coping with Chicago's problems, particularly with regard to judicial, police, fire, and sanitation services. A parallel problem was the increasing disparity between the growth and needs of Chicago and those of the rest of the state. Chicago was the disproportionate leader in the state's industry. In 1870 the gross value of manufactured products in Cook County totalled $92 million; the next highest county, with a total of $8 million, was Peoria.[4] Cook County political and business leaders headed the call for constitutional change which they hoped would provide solutions to Chicago's particular problems and a framework for continued expansion and specialization of functions. They were joined in demands for a new role for the state by commercial and agricultural groups whose unhappiness over the conduct of railroads had led them to demand that the state protect the public interest through some form of railroad regulation.

Illinois was not the only industrial state at this time to look to constitutional revision as a way to remedy crucial problems. In 1867 New York wrote a new constitution. Although it was rejected by the voters, many changes were later adopted by amendment, including

[2] Adlai E. Stevenson, "The Constitutional Conventions and Constitutions of Illinois," *Transactions of the Illinois State Historical Society* (1903), p. 26.

[3] U.S., Bureau of the Census, *A Compendium of the Ninth Census of the United States* (1870), pp. 8, 444–45; Bessie L. Pierce, *History of Chicago,* vol. 2, *From Town to City, 1848–1871* (New York: Alfred A. Knopf, 1940), p. 482.

[4] Ernest L. Bogart and Charles M. Thompson, *The Industrial State, 1870– 1893,* vol. 4 of The Centennial History of Illinois (Chicago: Illinois Centennial Commission, 1922), pp. 392–93.

a stronger role for the executive through an item veto. Michigan too held a constitutional convention in 1867, and its document also failed to get voter approval.[5] Illinois's situation in 1869 was somewhat more promising: convergence of the desire for reform by both Chicago and downstate groups, the widespread support of newspapers throughout the state, and the growing unmanageability of the legislature opened greater possibilities for the success of constitutional change.

The first move towards calling a fourth constitutional convention came in Governor Richard Oglesby's message to the newly convened legislature on January 7, 1867. Oglesby recommended a referendum at the next regular election on the question of calling a constitutional convention. He apparently thought it politic not to discuss the mass of private bills passed by the legislature as a reason for a new constitution. Instead, among the defects of the 1848 constitution he mentioned were legislative sessions restricted by salary limitations to forty-two days, insufficient number of senators and representatives, inadequate judicial system, obsolete two mill tax, and low salaries for state officials.[6] Following the governor's recommendations, the General Assembly passed a joint resolution to submit a convention call to the electorate.

The proposed call obtained immediate newspaper support. In fact, there was such impatience for a convention that the *Chicago Tribune* and other newspapers favored ignoring the law and holding the election of delegates at the same time as the convention referendum. The hope was that delegates could be elected in April, meet in June, and prepare a constitution for ratification in September, which would go into effect in January 1868. Although this plan came to nothing, the *Illinois State Journal,* in speaking favorably of it, claimed that "the need of a revision of the constitution is so pressing that there is a disposition even to strain a point, in order to attain the end."[7] However, despite such strong newspaper support

[5] Charles Z. Lincoln, *The Constitutional History of New York* ..., 5 vols. (Rochester: The Lawyers Co-operative Publishing Co., 1906), 2:339–43; D. R. Shilling, "The Michigan Constitution of 1908, or Constitution Making Since 1850," *Michigan History Magazine* 18 (1934):33–47.

[6] Illinois, Senate, *Journal,* 1867, p. 39.

[7] *Illinois State Journal,* January 3, 1867.

for a convention call, the voters approved it at the general election on November 3, 1868, by a majority of only 726 votes.[8]

SELECTION OF DELEGATES

The delegates were to be chosen at the general election in November 1869 and the convention was to meet in Springfield in that December. The 1848 constitution specified that the number of delegates equal the number of state representatives, eighty-five at that time. They would be paid six dollars a day while the convention was in session.[9] Some efforts were made to avoid the partisanship which marred the convention of 1862. Several candidates from Cook County organized themselves into a bipartisan People's party. Former State Supreme Court Judge John D. Caton of Ottawa declined the Democratic nomination for delegate with these words:

A constitution for a state, which must be a permanent, fundamental law, that may be expected to outlive party questions, should be founded upon a broader base than can be afforded by the platform of any party. Party predilections, interests and biases should be quite forgotten, and only the general permanent good should be allowed an influence in a constitutional convention. I had hoped that both parties would be influenced by these considerations, and would have elected men without party consideration. . . .[10]

Many partisan newspapers, however, rejected nonpartisan efforts. The Republican *Chicago Evening Post* stressed the importance of sending to the convention men capable of framing a constitution "Republican in all its features." The *State Journal* criticized the Chicago effort as a "mongrel ticket," sure to make trouble for the Republican party, while the *State Register* urged election of Democratic delegates who would insert into the constitution specific prohibitions against black suffrage in Illinois.[11]

The November 2, 1869, vote for delegates resulted in the election

[8] Illinois, Senate, *Journal*, 1869, 1:470.
[9] This enabling legislation can be found in *Laws of Illinois*, 1869, p. 222, and in the *Debates of the Convention* (1869–70), 2:1893.
[10] *Illinois State Register*, October 6, 1869.
[11] *Illinois State Journal*, October 13, November 3, 1869; *Illinois State Register*, November 1, 1869.

of almost an equal number of Republicans and Democrats.[12] The entire nonpartisan People's party ticket was elected in Cook County, and this delegation held the balance of power at the convention. Outside Cook County, however, the delegates reflected the sectional division of Illinois along party lines. The entire delegation from southern Illinois, with two exceptions, was Democratic, as was the west central delegation. All but four of the Republican delegates came from the northern and east central counties.[13] This sharp sectional cleavage of party representation was one of the problems taken up at the convention.

The delegates who assembled at the capitol building in Springfield on December 13 were a varied group which included, like earlier conventions, some of the most distinguished legal authorities and politicians in the state. Among the most prominent and active of these was Orville H. Browning, once a Whig and later a Republican, a close friend of Abraham Lincoln, U.S. Senator from 1861 to 1863, and secretary of the interior and acting attorney general under Andrew Johnson from 1866 to 1869.[14] By the time of the convention his conservatism and opposition to black suffrage had led him to reject party affiliations on either side. Reuben Benjamin from Bloomington, an authority on constitutional law, played an important role in the convention. He was credited with revising the bill of rights and was instrumental in bringing the convention around to favoring restriction of railroad corporations.[15] One of the best-known convention members was Joseph Medill, Republican party founder, Chicago delegate to the convention, and former editor and part owner of the *Chicago Tribune*.[16] With Medill's participation,

[12] Some discrepancy exists as to the exact party affiliation of the delegates. Bogart and Thompson, in *The Industrial State,* list 44 Democrats, 43 Republicans, and one Independent, totalling the 85 originally elected plus 3 later elected to fill vacancies. Illinois, Secretary of State, Edward Rummel, comp., *The Illinois Hand-Book of Information for the Year 1870* (Springfield, 1870), listed 43 Republicans, 36 Democrats, 3 Independent Democrats, one Independent, and one, Orville H. Browning, with no party affiliation (pp. 176–78). Whatever the exact makeup, it is obvious that the two parties were nearly equal in strength.

[13] *Illinois Hand-Book,* pp. 129–32.

[14] Newton Bateman, ed., *Historical Encyclopedia of Illinois,* 2 vols. (Chicago: Munsell Publishing Co., 1900), 1:63.

[15] Bogart and Thompson, p. 19.

[16] Bateman, 1:368.

the convention was assured of the support of at least one powerful newspaper in the state.

Elliott Anthony, Chicago lawyer, was also active in the convention proceedings. He was later the author of *The Constitutional History of Illinois,* and had been a member of the 1862 convention. One delegate, John Tincher of Danville, was currently serving as a state senator in the Twenty-sixth General Assembly, and two current state representatives, L. D. Whiting and Jonathan Merriam, also served as delegates.[17]

For the first time at an Illinois constitutional convention the overwhelming majority of the delegates, fifty-three of the original eighty-five, were lawyers. Whereas farmers had outnumbered lawyers in 1847, now lawyers outnumbered farmers by more than four to one. The lawyers as a group were younger than the men in other occupations; twenty-five of the thirty delegates under forty were lawyers. This indicated a trend in Illinois toward constitutions framed almost exclusively by members of the legal profession. The other members, who had felt competent to consider changes in the constitution despite their lack of legal training, were a declining group.[18]

The birthplace of the delegates also showed that change had taken place in Illinois's population makeup since the 1847 convention. The number of natives of the southern states of Kentucky, Tennessee, and Virginia declined from more than one-third of the convention in 1847 to less than one-fifth in 1869. The number of natives of the New York and New England areas increased proportionately. The fact that only eleven members were native Illinoisans indicates the continuing westward movement of U.S. population.[19] Although 20 percent of the state's population was foreign-born, only five delegates to the convention were naturalized citizens, two originally from England, two from Scotland, and one, Joseph Medill, from Canada. German and Irish immigrants in the state at that time numbered over 400,000,[20] but no representative from either of these groups was elected to the convention, and few of their particular problems were considered in its proceedings.

[17] *Illinois Hand-Book,* pp. 63–64, 176–78.
[18] In 1818, only five delegates had legal training.
[19] *Illinois Hand-Book,* pp. 176–78.
[20] In 1870 there were 515,198 foreign-born Illinois residents. These included 203,758 Germans and 192,960 from the British Isles, mostly Irish. *Compendium of the Ninth Census,* p. 392.

CONVENTION PROCEEDINGS

When the elected convention members assembled in Springfield on December 13, 1869, the principle of nonpartisanship received an immediate test in the fight over a temporary chairman. Downstate Republicans who wished to organize the convention on a party basis proposed William Cary from Galena. Democrats, who lacked the power to dominate a partisan convention, and Cook County Republicans backed John Dement, an "old pioneer" who had lived in Illinois when it was a territory and was now attending his third constitutional convention. A voice vote was taken, and since no one was yet qualified to rule on the vote, both were declared elected, both proceeded to the front of the hall and attempted to take the chair, and both ruled on motions for an hour or so. The principle involved was important enough that each man refused to give up the chair, although the whole matter was treated with laughter and good will. Finally nonpartisanship won out, and John Dement was elected temporary chairman by a vote of 44 to 32.[21]

The maneuverings over organization of the convention continued with the election of a permanent chairman. The bipartisan Cook County delegation had decided to put forward Republican Charles Hitchcock since the state was overwhelmingly Republican, and then to alternate the other offices between the two parties.[22] In opposition to this plan the downstate Republicans nominated Joseph Medill for permanent chairman. Hitchcock was elected by a narrow vote, 45 to 40, so the nonpartisan plan was followed. A Democrat, John Q. Harman of Cairo, was elected secretary; a Republican, Daniel Shepard of Chicago, was elected first assistant secretary; a Democrat was elected second assistant, and so on.[23]

For two reasons bipartisan organization and conduct was particularly important in the convention's success: first, for general public approval, since the public preferred to feel that convention delegates and their written work were above party considerations,

[21] All those voting for Cary were downstate Republicans who wished to organize the convention on a party basis. *Debates of the Convention* (1869–70), 1:1–6.

[22] Elliott Anthony, *The Constitutional History of Illinois* (Chicago: Chicago Legal News Print, 1891), p. 116.

[23] Most votes for officers carried by a narrow margin as downstate Republicans continued to resist the plan. *Illinois Hand-Book,* p. 174; *Debates of the Convention* (1869–70), 1:51–52.

and second, because an obviously partisan constitution would have alienated at least one major group in the state, the losing party. The passage of each constitution in Illinois has depended on avoiding the strong hostility of any major state group. Furthermore, the 1869 convention's bipartisan organization instilled a mood of conciliation and compromise into the convention at a time when feelings between the parties on a national level were bitter; Reconstruction continued under the Grant administration and the controversial Fifteenth Amendment was in the process of being ratified.

The split between Chicago and downstate was also patched over as much as possible. Both areas strongly desired constitutional change and realized that the public would be alienated by overt disagreements. Perhaps most important in mitigating Chicago-downstate schisms was the peculiar party alignment in the convention. The relatively equal party alignments meant that the Cook County delegation, elected on a nonpartisan basis, held the balance of power, and neither party could afford to alienate it.

After the election of a temporary chairman for the convention, fully three and one-half days were taken up with a discussion of which oath to take, the same question which had so bothered convention members in 1862. The long, serious, and sometimes bitter debate over what seems to be a trivial issue actually was pertinent, since in the process the questions of the function of a convention and a constitution were raised and analyzed.

The 1869 General Assembly's enabling act had specifically stated that members were to swear "to support the Constitution of the United States, and of this State." However, James Allen of Crawford County, who was to become extremely active in the convention, brought up the familiar point from the 1862 convention that the members could hardly in good faith swear to support the state constitution when they were gathered to change or rewrite it. William H. Underwood replied that he, as a member of the House of Representatives, had supported the oath provision in the enabling act because past experience had shown what convention members might do with their extraordinary powers if they did not first declare their allegiance to certain principles and controls as expressed in the state constitution. He specifically cited the Lecompton Constitution in Kansas and the efforts of the Illinois convention in 1862 as examples.[24]

Some of the members still subscribed to the philosophy of the 1862 convention. Delegate William Archer described a convention as "an elementary body, deriving its authority from no source; absolute sovereignty and paramount authority were the attributes of such a body; . . . it was, as it were, the people *en masse.*" Archer, who had been a member of the 1847 convention, recalled that at that time it was considered necessary to swear to support only the U.S. Constitution, and not that of the state.[25]

However, the majority of the members either did not agree with Archer's definition of the powers of the convention or, remembering the mistakes of 1862, feared public disapproval of such a definition as well as the time lost in debating the point. At first, the delegates agreed on a compromise resolution offered by Orville H. Browning, which would have modified the wording of the oath. However, on the fourth morning they overturned this decision in a stormy session during which at least one member walked out. It was finally agreed to make the oath prescribed by the legislature voluntary; a portion of the members took the oath and the convention proceeded to other business.[26]

A committee on rules was appointed. Its members reported the next day, having based their rules almost entirely on the work of the 1862 rules committee. Thirty-four standing committees were appointed to consider in working sessions the various sections to be changed or inserted into the constitution.[27] Much of the convention's time was spent in quarrels over details — such as the provision of postage stamps and stationery for the delegates — and in debates over mischievous resolutions. These time-wasting trivialities contributed to making the convention session the longest in Illinois constitution making to that time; the convention adjourned on May 13, 1870, after having been in session five months.

[24] *Debates of the Convention* (1869–70), 1:10–11. The entire debate over the oath is found on pp. 7–49.

[25] Ibid., 1:8.

[26] Ibid., 1:49.

[27] For a list of these committees as well as the members of each party and their affiliations, see *Illinois Hand-Book,* pp. 179, 180, 182.

Constitution of 1870

The constitution produced by the convention was longer and more detailed than earlier constitutions, signifying the growth in complexity of state needs and problems, and the intent of the constitution makers to continue the function of the constitution as an instrument of legislative policy as well as a statement of fundamental principles. In its excessive detail of matters best left to statute the Illinois constitution resembled its predecessor of 1848 and its contemporaries in other states. Many of the restrictions of the 1848 constitution were removed, but others, as often superfluous as harmful, were inserted into the new document. At the same time the delegates intended the constitution to be the embodiment of fundamental principles of government, as indicated by the obstacles to amendment included in the document. Despite alterations and excessive tampering with legislative matters, the convention delegates made no real effort to explore and change the basic structure of government; no changes were even considered for the existence and roles of the three branches of government, the groups they represented, or the financing of the state.

Many of the articles of the constitution, including the preamble, the boundaries article, and bill of rights, were essentially unchanged from the constitution of 1848. Under the leadership of Judge Benjamin, the archaic language in some sections of the bill of rights was streamlined and clarified.[28] Section 5 was modified to guarantee the right of trial by jury, and to permit a jury of less than twelve men in civil trials before justices of the peace. Few other changes of any substance were made from the 1818 and 1848 versions.

More constitutional changes were effected with regard to the legislature. The convention members lowered age requirements for representatives and senators, removed the restrictions on salaries imposed in the 1848 constitution, and strongly prohibited the collecting of special fees, thus accomplishing some of the popular purposes for which the convention was called. The number of senators was increased from 25 to 51, and the number of representatives from 85 to three times the number of senators, or 153. The representatives

[28] "The Four Constitutional Conventions of the State of Illinois," *Journal of the Illinois State Historical Society* 11 (1918):231.

were to be elected either from single-member districts or from multi-member districts by a process of cumulative voting, also termed minority representation.[29]

Minority representation was an attempt to solve the problem in Illinois political history of the geographical division between the Republican and Democratic parties in the state. In 1870, almost every legislative district in southern and western Illinois was Democratic, and the Republicans dominated the eastern and northern sections of the state. This situation, besides making effective legislation for the whole state difficult, had the result of virtually disenfranchising minority party voters in the state legislature. Allowing for the few minority representatives from each section, there remained of those who voted in the 1868 presidential election over one hundred thousand northerners voting for the Democratic candidate who were unrepresented by a Democrat in the House, and over fifty thousand southern Illinois Republicans similarly unrepresented by a Republican.[30] This problem had been discussed in newspapers and speeches, and the convention was expected to examine the matter.

The first move came on December 17 when Robert Hanna of Wayne County offered a resolution suggesting that the proper committee should consider the advisability of recommending a plan for giving the minority party in each district a chance to elect its candidate. This suggestion was followed through by the committee on electoral and representative reform, headed by Joseph Medill, which suggested the plan of cumulative voting. It provided that each voter "may cast as many votes for one candidate as there are representatives to be elected" — in this case three in each district — so that a candidate could receive from each voter either one, one and one-half, or three votes. This plan had received a great deal of attention in Europe, as well as in the United States; John Stuart Mill had endorsed it, and it had been put into practice in some of the Swiss cantons and in a few municipal elections in Pennsylvania. If ap-

[29] Verlie, pp. 111–12, 170–71.

[30] Of the 85 members of the 1869 House of Representatives of the Illinois General Assembly, only 8 of the 60 Republicans were from south of Springfield, and only 5 of the 25 Democrats represented districts north of that line. George Blair, "The Adoption of Cumulative Voting in Illinois," *Journal of the Illinois State Historical Society* 47 (1954):373, 375.

proved in Illinois, this would be the most extensive trial of cumulative voting yet held.[31]

Medill praised this proposed experiment, calling it "the only true democratic plan of representation," and claiming that it would "secure representation for our long enduring Republican friends in Democratic Egypt ... and the swallowed-up and buried-under Democrats of northern Illinois." While other convention members were not so enthusiastic, perhaps suspecting that Medill's real purpose was not reform but the perpetuation of Republican dominance in the state, they were desperate for some measure which might result in a better-quality legislature for the state, and by a vote of 46 to 17 chose to put the minority representation plan separately on the ballot.[32]

The convention, considering itself more representative of the people than the legislature was, attacked one of the legislature's major vices — the matter of private bills. The delegates made the passage of bills more difficult by requiring that all without exception be read on three different days and by forbidding the General Assembly to legislate on twenty-three specific subjects which had previously taken up so much of its time. Proscribed were such measures as granting divorces, regulating county and township affairs, incorporating cities, towns, or villages, regulating the rate of interest on money, and other similar matters, summed up with a general declaration that "in all other cases where a general law can be made applicable, no special law shall be enacted." The legislature was forbidden to "release or extinguish, in whole or in part, the indebtedness, liability, or obligation of any corporation or individual to this State or to any municipal corporation," thereby closing the door on one practice where the temptation to accept graft or bribery was obvious.

To judge from newspaper accounts, the delegates' action was wholeheartedly approved by the public. Also popular were the instructions to the legislature to enact certain laws, usually in response to petitions from organized groups. As in 1862, the General Assembly was ordered to pass "liberal Homestead and Exemption laws," as well as to legislate for greater safety in mining and for the

[31] *Debates of the Convention* (1869–70), 2:1726–27.
[32] Ibid., 2:1726–29.

establishment of private and public roads, though the value of inserting constitutional instructions to the legislature to pass good laws is questionable. Because of the controversy over the expense of the new capitol building in Springfield, the delegates included in the legislative article a declaration that the General Assembly was to limit the cost of the building to $3.5 million unless more funds were approved by referendum.

During the writing of the executive article, the convention members worked closely with Governor John M. Palmer, who enjoyed excellent relations with the delegates, in contrast to Governor Yates in 1862. The governor, himself a member of the 1847 constitutional convention, encouraged and supported the work of the delegates in 1870, both during the writing of the constitution and during the campaign for its passage. The convention members, in turn, respected the governor's ability enough to ask that all his veto messages be published so that they could be studied for recommendations for constitutional change. Undoubtedly, their respect for Palmer aided the delegates in their decision to give the governor more constitutional power. The governor was given the power to remove as well as to appoint state officials, and a stronger veto, which could be overturned only by two-thirds of the members elected to each house, a provision which had been defeated by the Whigs in 1848 and adopted by the Democrats in 1862.

The stronger veto was also included because of the trouble the governor had during the 1869 legislative session. In an attempt to restrain the passage of private and special laws, Palmer had vetoed seventy-two of the twelve hundred private laws passed at the session. The General Assembly repassed seventeen of these by a simple majority; most could not have been repassed if a two-thirds majority had been required.

The convention's action in giving the governor a stronger veto was in accord with the general trend toward increasing the power of the executive. Also in accordance with this trend, the restriction of the governor to one four-year term was removed, though not without extensive debate.[33]

The chief members of the executive department, the lieutenant

[33] Ibid., 1:153, 760–74; 2:1371–73.

governor, secretary of state, auditor, treasurer, attorney general, and superintendent of public instruction, remained as elective officers, although at least one convention member objected to the inclusion of the superintendent of schools in this group, since "the qualification of that officer, . . . depends on his education and upon his experience in the whole matter of schools and teaching. . . ." Perhaps specification of the election of the superintendent on a different date from that of other executive officers was an attempt to remove him from partisan politics.[34] Great suspicion was voiced during the convention debates about the temptations open to the treasurer, and therefore his term was restricted to two years.

The convention's deliberations over the amount of power which should be given to the legislature to amend or change municipal charters exposed the patched-over schism between Chicago and downstate delegates. Chicago delegates realized that in many cases Chicago's situation could not be covered by general municipal laws, and that special laws in regard to Chicago's problems were necessary; on the other hand they had no clear-cut theory of how home rule could best be effected. Therefore the rural and downstate bias against giving special consideration to Chicago won out, and a prohibition on any special legislation with regard to municipal charters remained. The 1870 debates on this issue clearly show that the delegates, like citizens of other states faced with the sudden appearance of large cities in an otherwise rural setting, were inexperienced and unwilling to deal pragmatically with the Cook County urban explosion.

This was also apparent with regard to the judiciary. While the entire state badly needed more and adequately-paid judges, Chicago's need was acute. The rapidly expanding economy and population of the city, and resultant expansion of litigation, had increased the need for both civil and criminal courts. And yet, special provision for the city's judicial system was greatly resented by some downstaters: one, John Tincher, echoed a common suspicion about urban life as he boasted that his own people in Vermilion County, "are a quiet, honest and industrious people, and do not require a judge for every forty thousand, as they do in those cities where there

[34] Ibid., 1:764.

are people who propose to live off of each other, by just peeling each other every time they pass upon the street."[35] Others also disliked the principle of discrimination between localities, but in this case admitted the realities of Chicago's judicial problems. The city was granted special criminal and superior courts, with one judge for every 50,000 people, while the rest of the state was divided into circuit courts, with one court for every 100,000 population. This system, though, provided too many trial courts with limited jurisdiction and was again to prove inadequate as Chicago continued to increase in population and complexity.

The delegates also increased the number of supreme court judges from three to seven, to be chosen from seven areas of the state for nine-year terms. All judges, including those of the supreme court, would continue to be popularly elected, a provision which aroused little debate at a time when the principle of popular election of state officials was still strong.

Suffrage was the focus of a great deal of attention in the 1869–70 convention, as both old and new suffrage controversies were debated. The committee on suffrage offered to the convention one majority and two minority reports: the majority report, eventually adopted, granted the franchise to male citizens over twenty-one who had resided in the state one year.[36] One of the minority reports reflected the newly reactivated woman suffrage movement, invigorated by the adoption of woman suffrage in the western territories of Wyoming in 1869 and Utah in 1870. Dormant during the war years, women's organizations in New York and Michigan had in the late 1860s attempted to gain the franchise by working through state constitutional conventions. Now in Illinois, petitions repeatedly calling for woman suffrage led to a request by four of the nine members of the suffrage committee, led by Elijah Haines of Lake County, to promote the submission of the woman suffrage question to the voters, and, if it was approved at the polls, to strike out the word "male" in the first section of the suffrage article.

Although some insisted that the ladies' "domestic cares and present

[35] Ibid., 2:1117.
[36] The franchise was also given to those who were electors in 1848, since until that year aliens had been able to vote. This continued a provision in the 1848 constitution. Ibid., 1:856.

field of action is broad enough and large enough to engage their whole time and attention, and we cannot afford to spare them from its sacred and solemn duties" for such a task as voting, the proposition received serious consideration from the convention members. In fact, in April 1870 the members voted 40 to 21 to submit the question of woman suffrage to the voters along with the constitution. However, in May, perhaps exasperated by suffrage leaders who allegedly advanced the theory that "men are out of their places in legislative halls, and on the judicial bench — that these places should be wholly given to women, and the men go to the fields and workshops,"[37] the convention members changed their minds and struck the woman suffrage proposition out of the proposed constitution schedule.[38]

Attempts were made to give the franchise to all male inhabitants of the state, and not to restrict it to citizens, evidence of a brief nationwide sentiment in the 1860s that aliens should have the vote.[39] All white male inhabitants had been allowed to vote in Illinois until the 1848 constitution had imposed a citizenship requirement, and the rejected 1862 constitution would have removed this qualification. In the debate over this question, however, John Dement and Joseph Medill led the majority in feeling that the foreign-born should not be given one of the major privileges of citizenship "without imposing any of the corresponding liabilities or duties upon them," and that this action would take away the inducement for them to become naturalized citizens. Medill further doubted that any state or nation had the right to extend voting privileges to anyone who still held allegiance to a foreign power. Those supporting the extension of the franchise to all inhabitants praised the intelligence of most foreign-born immigrants, and many called it an inconsistency to grant the franchise to blacks and not to foreign-born whites.[40]

[37] Quoted by L. D. Whiting, who was sympathetic to the woman suffrage cause, and was pleading with the members not to let suffrage leaders' speeches prejudice them against extending suffrage to women. Ibid., 2:1726.

[38] The vote was close — 33 to 28, with 22 absent or not voting. Votes on woman suffrage followed no particular political or sectional pattern, except that the proposal was consistently opposed by the Cook County delegation. Ibid., 2: 1726; 1309.

[39] Chilton Williamson, *American Suffrage from Property to Democracy, 1760–1860* (Princeton: Princeton University Press, 1960), p. 277.

[40] *Debates of the Convention* (1869–70), 2:1285–93.

As had been expected, some convention delegates attempted to counteract the effects of the Fifteenth Amendment to the United States Constitution, which had been approved and was to become effective as of March 30, 1870. The second minority report to the suffrage committee, written by three southern Illinois committee members, recommended submitting to the voters the question of whether or not the word "white" should remain in the suffrage article, as it had in previous constitutions. While some advocated this be resolved by public referendum, and supported a "white man's vote for a white man's government,"[41] federal action had by this time resolved the issue, and most convention members were not inclined to renew old bitterness and differences on racial issues, as had occurred in 1847. Less debate was held on this issue than on that of woman suffrage, and most convention members agreed with Joseph Medill that the state constitution now had "nothing to do with the right of the colored man to vote," that it was "not in the power of this convention to take it away from him." More discussion on the black's place in Illinois occurred when restrictions against blacks serving in the militia were removed. Several motions which would have specified segregation of colored from white troops were voted down.[42]

State constitutional provisions often bear little relationship to the activities of state government. In 1870 this was clearly true of education: though no mention of education had appeared in Illinois constitutions to that time, a statewide system of public education was already in operation. One delegate pointed out that the total sums raised for education in 1869 amounted to over $7 million — more than the entire revenue of the state government.[43]

Still, the delegates felt that some statement on education should be made in the constitution; most northern state constitutions in the 1850s and 1860s and the Reconstruction constitutions of the southern states had recognized the responsibility of state governments in this area. Therefore the Illinois General Assembly was instructed to

[41] Statement by O. H. Wright. Wright also did not propose to give the vote to "those pig-tailed fellows." Ibid., 2:1291.

[42] A resolution to commend the legislature's ratification of the Fifteenth Amendment carried by a straight party vote, 38 Republicans for, 36 Democrats against. Ibid., 1:165–66.

[43] Ibid., 1:767.

"provide a thorough and efficient system of free schools, whereby all children of this State may receive a good common school education." This statement was not arrived at without some heated debate: members from northern counties, whose proportion of taxable property was greater than their proportion of school children, were reluctant to appropriate funds for education from across the entire state and apportion them among the counties according to school population. However, James Allen of Crawford County and other southern members argued convincingly that "the well-being of the children was the concern of the state rather than of individual counties." The delegates apparently agreed, for they instituted the principle of equalization in state support of common school education.

The delegates assumed that their broad declaration of principle would assure education for children of all races in the state, but James M. Washburn introduced a resolution which would have submitted to a public vote the question of providing separate schools for white and colored children, and stated "that it is impolitic and unjust to appropriate any part of the taxes paid by the colored people of this State to the education of white children of the State and that it is equally impolitic and unjust to appropriate any part of the taxes paid by the white people of the State to the education of the colored people of the State." Washburn's resolution, however, was tabled the next day and the convention took no further action on school segregation. As a result of the provision for the education of all children, school boards immediately made arrangements for the education of hundreds of black children where this had not been previously provided; however, for decades pockets of school segregation remained in Illinois.[44]

Another controversy arose when a section was offered to the education article providing that "no teacher, State, county, township or district school officer shall ever be interested in the sale, proceeds or profits of any book, apparatus of furniture, used or to be

[44] Illinois, Superintendent of Public Instruction, *Eighth Biennial Report, 1869–70* (Springfield, 1870), pp. 25–29. Debate on this issue in the convention was on a party and sectional basis: those voting against tabling the resolution for segregated schools were Democrats, most from southern Illinois. *Debates of the Convention* (1869–70), 1:679, 703.

used, in any school in this State." Some delegates pointed out that this was class legislation against teachers — "a humble class, but a very worthy one," according to Elliott Anthony — and that it would prevent teachers from writing textbooks for use in the schools, but the measure was eventually included in the constitution.[45]

The line between church and state was clearly drawn, as section 3 of Article VIII prohibited any use of public funds in aid of church or sectarian schools, although it was pointed out in debate that thousands of children were attending parochial schools in Chicago while their parents were being taxed for the support of public schools.[46] A great deal of impassioned discussion took place concerning a proposal to permit Bible reading in the public schools. James G. Bayne of Woodford introduced a section instructing the General Assembly to "effectually prevent school officers . . . from excluding the Bible from said schools." Bayne supported his proposal by declaring that the Bible "is the only book now extant in the world by which man can have any definite idea of his origin or his creation." Bayne was opposed, however, by William H. Snyder of St. Clair who described the imposition this would be on the Catholics in the state, and by W. H. Underwood, who felt Biblical instruction should take place in the family, Sabbath school, and church, but that it had no place in the common schools. Joseph Medill pointed out that neither the federal constitution nor the constitutions of any of the other states carried such a provision, and the education article was completed without a reference to the use of the Bible in the public schools.[47]

The state of Illinois was in comparatively healthy financial condition at the time the convention met in 1869–70, and the revenue section of the constitution provoked little debate. There had been little demand for revision of the 1848 revenue sections, and these were left basically the same. The delegates dropped the two mill tax of 1848, removed the permit for a poll tax, greatly increased the list of objects which could be specially taxed by the legislature, and placed limits upon tax rates for county purposes and upon local

[45] Ibid., 2:1732–35.
[46] Ibid., 1:617–27.
[47] Ibid., 2:1739–45, 1751, 1758.

indebtedness, but they left the property tax as the basic measure for taxation in Illinois.[48]

In the area of corporation and railroad legislation, the delegates effected substantial change in constitutional provisions. The convention attempted again, as in 1848, to curb the legislature, after the latter's sorry role in the years before the convention. In the 1867 session, the legislature had organized by special charter, twenty-five banking institutions, two loan and trust companies, and seventy-two insurance companies which were permitted to borrow and loan money. During the following session in 1869, charters were granted by private laws to sixty-seven banks, fourteen loan and trust companies, and fifty-six insurance companies. No provisions were made in the charters for reports by the corporations to any state officer, or any other means for inspection of these and already-existing financial institutions.[49]

These abuses were to be corrected by restrictions on the legislature and by section 1 of Article XI which forbade the creation of a corporation, or the extension, change, or amendment of its charter, by special laws. Section 5 indicated that, as in 1862, there was very little enthusiasm for state banks: they were forbidden, and the state was forbidden to own stock in any bank. While this and other provisions were hostile and restrictive to state-chartered banks, the convention did not go so far as to abrogate existing bank charters or to forever prohibit notes and paper money in the state, as the 1862 convention had.

Another provision forbade the General Assembly to pass laws granting the right to construct and operate street railroads without local consent. This measure was an obvious reference to the notorious "ninety-nine year act" passed under suspect circumstances in 1865 to extend for ninety-nine years the charters of each of the three street car corporations then operating in Chicago. The bill was speeded through the House and passed, 66 to 3, then read in the Senate three times in one day and passed the same day, 19 to 4. After Governor Oglesby responded to a public uproar against the bill and vetoed it,

---

[48] During the decade after the constitution was adopted about 90 percent of state taxes were derived from the general property tax. Bogart and Thompson, pp. 310–11.

[49] Ibid., pp. 267–68.

the legislature promptly passed it over his veto.[50] The 1869–70 convention could not abrogate the ninety-nine year law, but it could hopefully prevent a reoccurrence of the circumstances of its passage by curbing the power of the legislature in this area.

Like earlier constitution writers, the delegates in 1870 forbid, in excessive detail, legislative actions favoring business and finanical organizations. By enacting these prohibitions time and time again, however, they tacitly admitted that demands on the legislature for such favors were unceasingly tempting and had to be guarded against in this way. In railroad legislation, however, the convention members broke new ground in defining the relationships between a state and a business operating within a state. Increasing pressure was levied on the delegates to take firm action against railroad abuses: groups as disparate as the Chicago Mercantile Association and *Prairie Farmer* magazine editors held farmer mass meetings and commercial conventions to mobilize public opinion for this purpose.[51]

During the first weeks of the convention, most of the delegates, while deploring the excessive and discriminatory rates charged by some of the railroad lines, felt that the state had no remedy for this situation except more competition, as explained by Robert P. Hanna:

> Build competing lines; hold out liberal inducements for capitalists to come from every portion of the country and invest their capital and compete with them. When you have done this, the problem is solved and the true and only relief furnished.

Joseph Medill agreed; while he admitted that "it is easy for gentlemen in their wrath to declare that railroad extortion must be stopped by law . . . I am not able . . . to conceive of any adequate and sufficient means of checking railroad cover charges and rapacity, by statute law of this State." However, continuing public pressure on the convention had its effect, and in the last month of the convention Reuben Benjamin, the respected authority on constitutional law from Bloomington, presented a carefully-reasoned argument, well

[50] Edward F. Dunne, *Illinois: The Heart of the Nation,* 5 vols. (Chicago: The Lewis Publishing Co., 1933), 2:200–201. Dunne was governor of Illinois from 1913 to 1917.

[51] Cole, *Era of the Civil War,* p. 358; Solon J. Buck, *The Granger Movement, 1870–1880* (Cambridge: Harvard University Press, 1913), pp. 128–52.

documented with court decisions, to the effect that the lawmaking body indeed had the right to regulate railroad rates. Since corporations had been created for the public good, and had been given the power of eminent domain, they were under the control of the legislature. Furthermore, the rights of private corporations ought not and could not stand in the way of public rights: "there are and can be no vested rights of governmental power in any individual or corporation, except those conferred by the constitution." Immediately after Benjamin's speech, Lewis Ross of Lewistown offered an amendment to the section on corporations giving the General Assembly the power to regulate rates.[52]

After a technical debate on the legal ramifications of this action, the convention members adopted several statements which carried out this principle. They declared that railroads are "public highways, and shall be free to all persons," and that the "General Assembly shall, from time to time, pass laws establishing reasonable maximum rates of charges for the transportation of passengers and freight on the different railroads in the State." The convention instructed the General Assembly to pass laws "to correct abuses and prevent unjust discrimination and extortion in the rates of freight and passenger tariffs on the different railroads in the state"; the enforcement of such laws could go as far as "forfeiture of their property and franchises."[53] The General Assembly would also have the authority to inspect the records of railroad corporations and to oversee their issuance of stocks and bonds. The convention then gave the General Assembly the same powers of inspection and regulation with regard to public grain warehouses.

Convention delegates decided to submit the provisions regarding railroads and the warehouses to the public separately from the body of the proposed constitution, so that their determination would not affect the fate of the entire constitution. Six other sections were also to be submitted separately: minority representation, the question of requiring a three-fifths vote to remove a county seat, an article on the formation of counties, and sections on the Illinois Central Rail-

[52] *Debates of the Convention* (1869–70), 1:325, 577; 2:1641–43.
[53] Democrats were more strongly in favor of railroad regulation than Republicans: 21 Democrats and 11 Republicans voted for the instructions to the General Assembly, and 23 Republicans and 4 Democrats voted against it. Ibid., 2: 1722.

road, restriction of municipal subscriptions to railroads, and the Illinois-Michigan Canal.

The Illinois Central Railroad held a unique tax status in Illinois. In the early 1850s the railroad had been authorized to build two lines totalling approximately seven hundred miles through the state and had received land grants as an incentive. In return for the grants and for exemption from other taxes the Illinois Central was to pay up to 7 percent of its receipts in to the state treasury. While some convention delegates wanted this exemption removed and the Illinois Central put on the same taxing basis as other railroads so that counties along the line could get benefits from its tax-exempt land and improvements, the majority wished to keep the system as it was. The convention therefore adopted a constitutional provision to insure that the railroad's special taxing position in the state could not be changed in the future without constitutional revision.

Also submitted separately was a provision that "no county, city, town, township or other muncipality, shall ever become subscriber to the capital stock of any railroad or private corporation, or make donation to or loan its credit in aid of, such corporation. . . ." Previously, many local areas had gone bankrupt or deeply into debt to attract a railroad line to their area. Although this provision was intended to prevent any more of these unfortunate ventures, one more had to be allowed. In the fall of 1869 the citizens of Quincy had subscribed to a railroad to be built across the river in Missouri, and construction had already begun. So the convention inserted a special lengthy exemption for Quincy in deference to its distinguished convention representative, Orville H. Browning.[54]

The Illinois-Michigan Canal issue was one of the first to be considered by the convention, and it aroused bitter Chicago-downstate antagonism. Downstaters felt the canal, which had opened for navigation in 1848 as the only successful project of the state's disastrous internal improvement system, was being run by the state purely for the benefit of Chicago, and many wished to give the state permission to sell or lease it if desired. Their opponents wanted instead to enlarge and improve the canal as a means of providing competition for high railroad rates. Finally, Orville Browning presented an

[54] Ibid., 2:1762–63.

approved compromise which provided that the canal could never be sold or leased without the legislature's first submitting the question to the voters at a general election and receiving majority approval for the action.[55]

A great deal of deliberation was given in the 1869–70 convention to the question of future constitutional conventions, and the delegates sought earnestly to avoid future controversies. They devoted most attention, though, to those matters which had proved troublesome to their own convention, namely, the number and replacement of delegates and the matter of the oath.

During the convention four delegates died and one resigned. Since no guidelines from 1848 had been established, and the members were not willing to accept the precedent of the much briefer 1818 convention that time was too short to elect replacements, the members decided after long debate that the convention had the power to order special elections for substitute members, and three of these elections were held during the convention.[56] To avoid a similar situation in any future convention, they decided that vacancies should be filled in the same manner provided for filling vacancies in the General Assembly.

The first big controversy of the convention had been the question of the oath to be taken by delegates. To avoid this in future conventions, the delegates provided explicitly that "before proceeding the members shall take an oath to support the Constitution of the United States, and of the State of Illinois, and to faithfully discharge their duties as members of the Convention." Many members still disputed this decision, since most delegates in 1869 had refused to take such an oath, but a majority felt the question should be decided in advance for future conventions.[57] Their action proved to be well-founded; the oath was not an issue in either the 1920 or the 1969–70 conventions.

One of the declared aims of the 1869–70 convention had been to make alteration of the Illinois Constitution easier, but in debating the amending process, the delegates reopened the conflict over

[55] Ibid., 1:310–20, 478. The canal was operated by the state until 1882, when the people voted to cede it to the national government as part of a lakes-to-the-gulf waterway. Bogart and Thompson, p. 347.
[56] *Debates of the Convention* (1869–70), 1:197–208.
[57] Ibid., 2:1312.

the role of state constitutions. A determined group attempted at first to make amendment easier than it was under the 1848 constitution, whose provisions were so detailed and time-consuming that no changes had been adopted. In the 1870 provisions, amendments could be proposed in either house of the General Assembly. If approved by two-thirds of all members elected to each house, they would be submitted to the voters at the next general election, and would be adopted if approved by "a majority of all the electors voting at said election." This provision for a majority of all those voting was not restrictive at a time when the parties printed their own ballots and simply included a constitutional question on the ballot. The voter would automatically follow his party's decision to vote for or against the amendment unless he took the trouble to scratch out the provision.[58]

The delegates restricted the General Assembly to proposing amendments to not more than one article in one legislative session, nor to the same article more often than every four years. This restriction was warmly debated by convention members. John Dement, who had by this time seen three conventions and favored an easier way of changing the constitution, argued for permission to allow at least two articles to be amended at one session and accused others of lack of faith in future voters, stating, "I do not feel so distrustful of the people, as to be afraid that, if the General Assembly should submit amendments to two articles at one session, and either of them, or both of them, should be objectionable, they would not have judgment enough to reject one or both of them, as the necessity might require." Dement was upheld in this view by Joseph Medill, Lewis Ross, and L. D. Whiting, who enumerated all the states whose constitutions contained no such restrictions on the number of amendments, nor the requirement of a four-year interval between amendments to one article. However, the majority evidently went along with a physician who feared that "we would have the Legislature, half of its time, perhaps, engaged in framing proposed amendments to the Constitution." George Wait of Geneseo predicted that if the legislature could propose two amendments to the constitution at one

[58] Illinois, Legislative Reference Bureau, *Constitutional Conventions in Illinois,* 2d ed. (Springfield, 1919), p. 34.

session, "the Legislature, in a very short time, could entirely demolish our Constitution, build up a new one on its ruins, and thus make our organic law as unstable as the desert sands." The attempt to allow two amendments at the same session failed by a vote of 24 to 21.[59]

The 1870 constitution writers could not have foreseen, of course, the changes in voting procedure which would make it so difficult after 1891 to get enough voters even to consider constitutional amendments, let alone approve them. Nor could they have known that the minority representation being introduced into the legislature would make a two-thirds vote for submitting an amendment extremely difficult to obtain. Nevertheless, it is clear from their debate that the members of the 1869-70 convention, despite their condemnations of the 1848 members and their determination not to follow the same example, were not immune to feeling that the product of their work should be, if not immortalized, at least well guarded from extensive change. The inclusion in the constitution of statutory material, which was then regarded as organic law above amendment, was one of the major handicaps of the 1870 constitution, contributing to great difficulties in Illinois state government.

The schedule for the constitution provided for its submission to the electorate, together with its eight separate sections, at a special election on the first Saturday in July 1870. The constitution was signed by seventy-nine members on May 13, and the convention adjourned the same day.

VOTER APPROVAL

During the seven-week period between adjournment of the convention and the special election, the proposed constitution was endorsed by almost all influential government figures and by the press. Governor Palmer wrote to a friend that he felt "no hesitation in saying that the interests of the people of the State demand the adoption of the proposed constitution," and that if the people should adopt the proposed constitution and send honest, independent men to the General Assembly, they might "firmly expect the reign of law

[59] *Debates of the Convention* (1869–70), 2:1314–18, 1592–95.

instead of the dominion of lobbyists and speculators in special privileges and in public taxation."[60]

The *Chicago Tribune* in an editorial stressed the bipartisan nature of the proposed document:

> Upon the whole, the new constitution is a great improvement upon the old. The single section prohibiting special legislation is of incalculable value, and ought to secure its ratification, even though it contained no other improvement upon the old . . . .

> There is not a single section or paragraph in the whole instrument of a partisan nature. There is no reason why a Republican would be more in favor of it than a Democrat, or a Democrat than a Republican. In this respect, the new constitution appeals to each man as a citizen and a taxpayer — as a member of a commonwealth that will live long after existing political parties are forgotten. We can see no reason, therefore, why it should not be cordially supported by men of all shades of political and religious belief.[61]

The *Tribune* claimed that "nearly the whole press of the State and the leading men of both parties, have pronounced in favor of the new constitution." The only opposition, it said, came from "professional bummers, lobbyists, and barnacles who oppose reform," from those who wished to build railroads financed by counties and towns, and from a few Democratic newspapers, such as the *Quincy Herald,* which were firmly opposed to black civil rights.[62]

Despite these few opponents, evidence shows that most public figures and newspaper editors agreed with the *Illinois State Journal,* which commented:

> No one, we are sure, can fail to observe how much better adapted to the present wants and necessities of the State the new Constitution is than the old. That such will be the judgment of the people upon the comparison, we most heartily trust and hope.[63]

[60] Letter from John M. Palmer to Jesse W. Fell, June 18, 1870. Jesse W. Fell Papers (transcripts in Illinois Historical Survey, Urbana).

[61] *Chicago Tribune,* May 13, 1870.

[62] The *Herald* asked the question, "Do you suppose a Radical legislature would establish separate schools for the Negroes, unless it was *required* by the constitution to do so?" *Quincy Herald,* as reprinted in the *Chicago Tribune,* June 23, 1870.

[63] *Illinois State Journal,* May 14, 1870.

The voters of Illinois also apparently agreed with this statement; the constitution was approved on July 2 by a large majority, 134,277 to 35,443, although the vote was light, less than half that for presidential elections in 1868 and 1872.[64] Party alignments were a factor only as they corresponded to sectionalism: eleven of the nineteen counties returning a vote against the constitution were Democratic, but all nineteen were in the southern half of the state, and included strong opposition from Adams, Pike, and Schuyler. Three central Illinois counties which returned favorable majorities for Democratic presidential candidates in 1868 and 1872, Sangamon, Macoupin, and Christian, registered sizeable votes in favor of the new constitution.[65] Cook County voters approved the constitution by the greatest margin, 22,239 to only 341 against, but even without the Cook County vote the constitution carried by a considerable majority.

The eight propositions submitted separately were also approved. Six of these were approved by greater margins than was the constitution itself, with the largest number of votes being cast for the section relating to the Illinois Central Railroad. The section on minority representation aroused the most opposition and received the narrowest favorable margin of votes, 99,022 to 70,080. This section was opposed by a majority of voters in forty Illinois counties, but was passed through large favorable votes in several northern counties, with Cook approving the minority representation proposal by a vote of 20,139 to 2,244.[66]

There were two main factors in the overwhelming approval of the new constitution. The first was the great public dissatisfaction with the performance of Illinois state government, linked with the widespread belief that changes in the state constitution would effect material improvements in this performance. Second, the constitution written by the convention was a bipartisan document which did

[64] An abstract of the vote on the constitution by counties is printed in the *Debates of the Convention* (1869–70), 2:1894–95. The voters in eighty-three counties favored the constitution while those in nineteen counties opposed it.

[65] W. Dean Burnham, *Presidential Ballots, 1836–1892* (Baltimore: Johns Hopkins Press, 1955), pp. 368–91.

[66] Other counties giving strong approval to minority representation included Bureau, Christian, Kane, Knox, La Salle, Macoupin, McLean, Whiteside, and Sangamon.

not arouse the opposition of any major segment of government or public opinion. For these reasons, even controversial proposals such as minority representation and state control over warehouses and railroads were approved. The constitution went into effect on August 8, 1870.

V

Constitutional Revision
1870–1946

IMPLEMENTATION OF THE 1870 CONSTITUTION

In the late nineteenth century Illinois's 1870 constitution was considered a reform document. Its acceptance of a regulatory role for the state in regard to railroads and warehouses was an idea whose time had come. Other state constitutions in the 1870s adopted variations of the Illinois provisions. Pennsylvania and California established railroad and canal regulation in new constitutions in 1873 and 1879, as did Ohio in its unsuccessful proposed constitution in 1873. Illinois was a model for constitutions of the new western states: Colorado's 1876 constitution provided state responsibility for mine regulation and irrigation, and the work of the Nebraska constitutional conventions of 1871 and 1875 showed the influence of Illinois's constitution of 1870. Although cumulative voting was never adopted by any other state, a South Dakota constitutional convention submitted the question to the voters in 1885. It was defeated by a vote of 15,765 to 11,273.[1]

Reform provisions in constitutions are only as effective as their implementation allow them to be. The 1870 Illinois Constitution gave guidelines for state government, but without major structural

[1] See Thorpe; see also, James C. Olson, *History of Nebraska* (Lincoln: University of Nebraska Press, 1955), pp. 187–90, and *Dakota Constitutional Convention Held at Sioux Falls, September, 1885* (1907) 1:47.

reform. Change depended on the same system and many of the same judges and legislators who had shown such disregard for the public concern before the 1869–70 convention. One by one, major provisions of the 1870 constitution were circumvented, ignored, or misapplied, through tortuous judicial interpretations and legislative action or inaction, with little notice by an apathetic public. Those few changes which were accomplished took place through constitutional amendments and through legislation which largely ignored the state constitution.

Only unceasing public vigilance immediately after the constitution's approval led to railroad and warehouse legislation to carry out the constitutional mandate. The 1871 General Assembly, after some prompting by commercial and agricultural interests, enacted the Railroad Act of 1871, which set standards for fair and uniform rates and created the Railroad and Warehouse Commission to carry them out. The commission was at that time an innovation; Massachusetts was the only state with a commission for railroad control, and Illinois's inclusion of warehouse regulation was unique. However, its effectiveness was another matter. The railroads followed the commission's orders to submit regular reports, but refused to institute the rates established by the commission, and when the commission indirectly instituted suits against the railroads, these were denied in the courts. Chief Justice Charles B. Lawrence announced a unanimous decision of the Illinois Supreme Court that the Railroad Act of 1871 violated the state constitution, though not the United States Constitution.[2]

This decision aroused angry protests throughout the state. Agricultural interests formed an Illinois State Farmers' Association which called a State Farmers' Convention in 1873 and created, together with commercial interests, a lobby to counterbalance the railroad lobby in Springfield. The legislature, heeding the direction of public opinion, passed the Railroad Law of 1873, which was stronger and removed the constitutional objections to the law of 1871. Justice Lawrence was defeated in his bid for reelection the same year, and judicial candidates favorable to railroad regulation did well at the polls. Attempts by the railroads to defeat the new legislation were

[2] Bogart and Thompson, pp. 91–94.

then denied in the Illinois courts. As a result, the United States Supreme Court, in its landmark decision *Munn* v. *Illinois* in 1877, declared that the state indeed had the power to regulate business affected with the public interest.[3]

After this success, though, organized pressure faded. The effectiveness of the state's regulation of railroad rates is difficult to evaluate. By the end of the century freight rates in Illinois were lower than those for the United States as a whole, but this was due to many factors. Illinois's railroad lines were largely completed by the mid-1870s and required less major capital investment than did railroads elsewhere. Improvements in equipment and management reduced costs and the state's central location in a nationwide traffic system contributed to the ability of its railroads to charge lower rates.[4] The creation of a commission for regulatory purposes did prove to be a more effective method than reliance on legislation alone, though the commission often established rates high enough to allow the railroads considerable latitude. The nationwide character of the system also hampered state regulation. The commission's main function soon became hearing and adjusting complaints. By 1893 the commission adopted rules of practice to govern the complaint procedure, and most disputes were settled without formal trial. The commission heard many complaints against discrimination or high charges for particular tasks such as switching loaded cars, but most complaints still concerned excessive rates, raising a doubt as to the overall effectiveness of regulatory legislation.[5]

In other areas, the intentions of constitution writers in 1869–70 were circumvented by public apathy or the legislators' continued willingness to succumb to the pleas of private interests. Cumulative voting did fulfill the goal of minority party representation for each section of the state, but the favoring of special interests was a nonpartisan matter. A majority of both Democrats and Republicans, for example, approved the Allen law in 1897 to grant fifty-year franchises to private streetcar corporations and to permit consolidation

[3] Buck, *Granger Movement*, p. 142.

[4] Ernest L. Bogart and John M. Mathews, *The Modern Commonwealth, 1893–1918*, vol. 5 of The Centennial History of Illinois (Springfield: Illinois Centennial Commission, 1920), pp. 119–24, 507.

[5] Illinois, Railroad and Warehouse Commission, *Report* (1893), pp. 6, 153–59; Ibid. (1899), p. xi.

of noncompeting companies. Governor John Peter Altgeld had vetoed similar legislation two years before, calling it "legalized monopoly."[6] The 1870 constitution writers had tried to guard against this action by stipulating that the consent of local authorities had to be obtained for any such measure. However, in the 1890s the Chicago city council combined with both parties in the legislature to favor traction monopolies in the city.[7]

After 1870 taxation also suffered from the disparity between constitutional stipulations and economic and political realities in the state. With the rise of intangible property holdings in the state, the property tax base of the taxing system had become inadequate and unfair. The legislature, subject to business pressure, undervalued commercial property for taxation and proved unwilling or unable to tax excess corporation profits adequately. The state board of equalization failed to adjust and fix equal and fair assessment rates within geographic areas or among occupational groups.[8] The general property tax was clearly unsatisfactory as the major source of state revenue, but the constitutional stipulation that taxation of property be uniform seemed to prevent any change.

Governor Altgeld considered the revenue situation to be the major problem calling for constitutional revision, as he stated in his inaugural address in 1893:

> There is a wide-spread conviction that the present revenue system of our State results in the greatest inequalities and injustice in the matter of taxation. . . . Various measures in relation to it will no doubt be presented to your consideration, the most important of which is, perhaps, the question whether any comprehensive change can be made without a revision of our Constitution. In the past, our State has revised its Constitution at intervals of thirty and twenty-two years.[9]

The Senate adopted a joint resolution to submit the question of holding a constitutional convention to the people in 1893. However,

---

[6] *Laws of Illinois*, 1897, pp. 282–85; Dunne, 2:213–21.

[7] Harvey Wish, "Altgeld and the Progressive Tradition," *American Historical Review* 56 (1940):823–24.

[8] Illinois, Revenue Commission, *Report* (1886), pp. 2–3; Robert M. Haig, *A History of the General Property Tax in Illinois*, University of Illinois Studies in the Social Sciences, vol. 3, nos. 1 and 2 (Urbana, 1914), pp. 147, 173.

[9] Illinois, House, *Journal*, 1893, p. 55.

members of the House of Representatives rejected the resolution on the last day of the legislative session, by a vote of 74 to 48. Six years later, a Cook County Republican senator introduced a similar resolution for a vote on calling a constitutional convention, but it never reached the floor of the Senate.[10]

Sentiments for a new constitutional convention were prompted in part by the unforeseen difficulties in revising the constitution through the amendment process. During the twenty years following adoption of the constitution of 1870, change by amendment was accomplished with relative ease, primarily because the use of the party ballot kept non-voting on amendments from becoming a serious impediment to obtaining the necessary majority of votes cast at the election.[11] From 1848 to 1891 each political party printed its own ballots and distributed them among the voters. The party committee or convention established the party's position on proposed amendments to the constitution. If the party favored the amendment, its ballots would include the phrase "For the proposed amendment of section _____ of Article _____ of the Constitution"; if the party opposed the amendment, the word "against" would be substituted for the word "for." In any event, the voter was bound by the action of his party unless he took the trouble to scratch out the phrase as printed. Under this system adoption or rejection of proposed constitutional amendments was controlled largely by party conventions or committees. A measure approved by both parties had no trouble getting the popular vote necessary for approval.[12] Under the party ballot system, the vote on proposed constitutional amendments often approximated the total number of votes cast in the election. From 1871

---

[10] Ibid., pp. 1184–85; Illinois, Senate, *Journal*, 1899, p. 44.

[11] The first amendment, passed in 1878, showed the new needs of the state. It instructed the assembly to pass laws regarding drainage ditches and other improvements which cut across the property of several owners. In 1880 an amendment prohibited county sheriffs or treasurers from succeeding themselves. An 1884 amendment gave the governor the power to veto items in appropriation bills without negating entire bills. The fourth amendment, passed in 1886, prohibited the hiring of convict labor. In 1890, because of constitutional prohibitions against municipal indebtedness, the constitution was amended to allow Chicago to issue $5 million worth of bonds to finance the World's Columbian Exposition in 1893. *Constitution of the State of Illinois and United States* (Springfield, 1967), p. 10.

[12] Illinois, Legislative Reference Bureau, *Constitutional Conventions in Illinois*, p. 34.

to 1891, five amendments were proposed and all were approved. The average rate of non-voting was only about 23 percent.

All this was changed in 1891 when the General Assembly passed an official ballot law instituting the Australian voting system. All propositions to be voted on were printed at the bottom of the official ballot with blank spaces for both favorable and unfavorable marks, but with no provision by which a straight party vote could count either for or against such propositions. The voter had to specifically mark each space or he failed to vote at all on that proposition, thereby counting his vote as a "no" vote on proposed constitutional amendments. Between 1892 and 1896 three amendments were submitted to the voters, including the first of the so-called "Gateway amendments" to liberalize the amending process. Each of these proposals was soundly defeated, primarily because 79 percent of the voters failed to mark their ballots on the question.[13]

The constitution also required that before they could be submitted to the voters proposed amendments must pass both houses by a two-thirds majority of all elected members. This was often difficult to achieve under cumulative voting, which guaranteed a permanently large minority in the House of Representatives.

Despite the difficulties in the amending procedure, however, most of Altgeld's reform supporters were unenthusiastic about a new constitutional convention. The Chicago Civic Federation, the Chicago Citizens' Association, and other reform groups continued to work through the amendment method for constitutional revision, which they hoped would remedy some of the evils of state government and of Chicago-downstate relations. After the first Gateway amendment failed in 1892, these groups tried to heighten voter awareness of constitutional propositions on the ballot by providing a separate "little ballot" for proposed constitutional amendments.[14] The major goal of

[13] This trend continued: from 1891 to 1950, only two of the fourteen amendments submitted to the voters were adopted by the required majority. Ten others were approved by large majorities of those voting on the question, but fell short of a majority of the total number of voters in the election. *Constitution of the State of Illinois and United States* (1967), p. 10.

[14] From 1899 to 1929 six proposals were submitted on the separate "little ballot." Of these, two amendments and a proposal to call a convention were approved. Ibid.; Illinois Legislative Council, *Constitutional Revision in Illinois,* Publication 85 (Springfield, 1947), p. 12.

this innovation was to get voter approval for a new home rule provision for Chicago.

During the last decades of the nineteenth century municipal home rule was the desire of numerous urban reform groups across the nation. The National Municipal League and other civic organizations wanted to release cities from the clutches of state legislatures as a first step in remedying the wastefulness, inefficiency, and corruption in urban government.[15] In 1904 Chicago business and professional reformers, with this goal in mind, were able to get an amendment passed on the "little ballot," which allowed the legislature to grant a limited home rule charter for Chicago. The measure was strongly supported by Governor Richard Yates and by both political parties.

Discussion of another constitutional convention for Illinois therefore abated in the first decade of the twentieth century. Progressive reformers throughout the United States were focusing attention on state, local, and municipal reform, but effected most of this through constitutional amendments. From 1901 to 1908 almost three hundred amendments to state constitutions were proposed, and 181 of these were adopted. Many were home rule measures, as in Illinois, while others incorporated various forms of the initiative and referendum as a means of increasing popular control over legislative, and in some cases judicial, decision making.[16]

Apart from the modest home rule provision passed in 1904, Illinois's record of constitutional change during the Progressive era is meager. Unlike neighboring Wisconsin, Ohio, and Iowa, state government in Illinois was not a major focal point of reform. The friction between Chicago and the rest of the state made change in Springfield extremely difficult. Downstate legislators who otherwise might have sympathized with improving local government rejected urban reforms for Chicago almost as a matter of policy. Chicago legislators themselves were divided on many issues. The reform goals of upper middle class business and professional leaders were not the

[15] *Hand Book of the National Municipal League, 1894–1904* (Philadelphia, 1904), p. 10.

[16] Michigan did adopt a new constitution in 1908 and Oklahoma's constitution as a new state in 1907 contained many progressive provisions. Walter F. Dodd, "Recent Tendencies in State Constitutional Development, 1901–1908," *Proceedings of the American Political Science Association* 5 (1908):149–50.

same as those of the machine politicians whose major source of strength was the immigrant vote. When these Chicago groups could get together, as they did under the leadership of Democratic Governor Edward F. Dunne between 1913 to 1917, they were able to join with downstate progressives in pushing reform legislation through the General Assembly.[17] Most of this legislation did not involve state constitutional provisions, however. Without reference to constitutional revision, the Dunne administration created a state public utilities commission to supersede the Railroad and Warehouse Commission, reorganized the State Highways Department, broadened the workmen's compensation law and passed an employers' liability act, granted women the right to vote on statutory offices and questions of public policy, and created a commission on efficiency and economy, a legislative reference bureau, an unemployment commission, and a conservation department. Governor Dunne himself advocated constitutional revision through a Gateway provision to increase the number of constitutional amendments which could be permitted at one time, but his efforts to bring such a question to the voters did not succeed.[18]

Dunne's failure was partly the result of ambivalence existing about constitutional reform. Most Illinois residents in the early twentieth century agreed that constitutional changes were needed, but it was difficult to determine what kinds, or how effective they would be. The constitutional amendment passed in 1904 had permitted the General Assembly to pass home rule legislation, but meaningful legislation was not forthcoming. Many downstate legislators tied home rule for Chicago to permanently limited representation for Cook County in any new reapportionment of the state legislature.

The reapportionment issue was the most bitter in state politics in the early twentieth century. As dictated by the 1870 constitution, the legislature reapportioned the state legislative and U.S. congressional districts following the 1880, 1890, and 1900 censuses, but failed to do so after the 1910 census. The legislature's failure to reapportion in

[17] John D. Buenker, "Urban Immigrant Lawmakers and Progressive Reform in Illinois," in *Essays in Illinois History in Honor of Glenn Huron Seymour,* ed. Donald F. Tingley (Carbondale: Southern Illinois University Press, 1968), pp. 52–53.
[18] Dunne, 2:424.

1911 could be traced to many factors. First was Chicago's continuing growth, faster than that of the state as a whole. According to the 1910 census, Chicago's population had reached the two million mark and was still growing.[19] Downstate legislators feared domination of the state by Chicago machine politics. Downstate residents exhibited the traditional fear of the wickedness, corruption, and political radicalism of the big city, shown particularly by the almost pathological hatred of Chicago newspapers by the public outside of Cook County. Those Chicago politicians who benefitted from the status quo also worked against reapportionment, as did Republican and Democratic party leaders who stayed in power by exploiting the urban-rural division, and lobbyists who had found the situation profitable.[20]

Attempts by Governor Dunne to force the legislature to reapportion the state were voted down, and Illinois courts refused to provide a remedy. In 1895, the Illinois Supreme Court had ruled that the courts did not have

> any power to compel the legislature to act in any case, ... so that if the legislature should wholly neglect or refuse to pass an apportionment act after the lapse of ten years, and should leave in force an act under which the districts have become grossly unequal in population, the people would have no remedy, outside of a constitutional amendment, except to elect a General Assembly which would perform the duty.[21]

The irritation of most Chicagoans at this violation of the constitution was increased by the inequality of the reapportionment in 1901, which carved districts in a Republican-favored gerrymander. Despite this clear violation of the principle of equal representation, the 1901 reapportionment was approved by the state supreme court.[22] For two reasons the apportionment situation made many reformers pessimistic about the chances for effective constitutional revision: first, any convention whose delegates were chosen on the

[19] U.S., Bureau of the Census, *Thirteenth Census* (1910), p. 74.

[20] Alex Elson, "Constitutional Revision and Reorganization of the General Assembly," *Illinois Law Review* 33 (1938):19–20.

[21] *People* v. *Thompson*, 155 Ill. 451 (1895), quoted in Illinois Legislative Council, *Legislative Apportionment in Illinois*, Publication 112 (Springfield, 1952), p. 5.

[22] Bogart and Mathews, p. 292.

basis of the 1901 reapportionment would be nonrepresentative of the population and weighted against Cook County, and second, if a constitutional directive could be disobeyed without judicial remedy, as in the case of reapportionment, what was the use of establishing constitutional mandates at all? A new constitutional convention could hardly force the legislature to reapportion the state or force the judiciary to make the legislature do it. In fact, to Chicagoans there was always the danger that a convention would establish Chicago as a permanent minority in state government by constitutionally restricting the number of legislative seats allowed it.[23] Therefore many progressive Chicago leaders were dubious about a constitutional convention.

MOVEMENT FOR A CONVENTION

Other Chicagoans and many downstate leaders felt that a convention and new constitution offered the only hope for correction of the worst abuses of Illinois government. Gradually they attracted more supporters for a movement toward that goal. In December of 1910, twenty Chicago civic organizations sent representatives to draw up a program for constitutional reform. This group proposed several constitutional amendments and endorsed the movement for a constitutional convention. In 1913 the Citizens' Association of Chicago urged the submission of the question to a popular vote. In 1914 the Constitutional Convention League was organized with a statewide board of directors and an advisory council and officers who were prominent in politics or interested in better government. In 1915 the Constitutional Convention League was replaced by a statewide constitutional convention committee of the Citizens' Association of Chicago, and this association continued to agitate for submission of a convention call to the voters.[24]

One impetus towards this growing support was the example of governmental reform in other states, and particularly the example of

[23] Charles LeRoy Brown, "Possibility of Illinois Being Divided into Two States," *Illinois Law Review* 7 (1912):32.

[24] Orrin N. Carter, "Unofficial Steps in Connection with the Calling of the Constitutional Convention of 1920," in *Delegates' Manual of the Fifth Constitutional Convention of the State of Illinois, 1920,* ed. B. H. McCann (Springfield, 1920), p. 63.

the Ohio constitutional convention of 1912. The Ohio convention
incorporated a number of progressive reforms in amendments,
among them an initiative and referendum provision, judicial reform,
strong municipal home rule, banking reform, mandatory civil service, a minimum wage, and workmen's compensation.[25] Another
factor was the shift in focus by national civic organizations from
attempts to reform municipal governments to a critical examination
of state government in terms of its morality, efficiency, and economy.
One of the revisions of state government suggested by the National
Municipal League was the short ballot, by which executive officers
would be appointed by the governor rather than popularly elected,
thereby streamlining the executive department. In 1914 in Illinois
the short ballot was advocated as a reason for a constitutional convention by the Citizens' Association of Chicago and the Constitutional Convention League.[26] The move toward a constitutional convention was initiated by Chicago and downstate business and civic
leaders and members of the legal profession — the conservative wing
of the progressive movement in Illinois. Labor leaders, immigrant
spokesmen, and machine politicians in Chicago, less confident that
the path to reform lay in governmental efficiency and constitutional
revision, were unenthusiastic about the calling of a convention.[27]

The results of the 1916 elections brought the convention call
nearer. First, any lingering hopes for revision through the amendment process were dampened by the defeat of a revenue amendment
to the constitution. Furthermore, Frank O. Lowden had been elected
governor. Lowden, progressive Chicago attorney and politician,
advocated a constitutional convention because it might bring efficiency and economy to state government.[28] His inaugural message to
the General Assembly on January 8, 1917, included a strong plea
for adoption of a convention call:

The time has come for a new State Constitution. The constitutions
framed since the Civil War, including our own, have not been

[25] Hoyt L. Warner, *Progressivism in Ohio, 1897–1917*. Columbus: Ohio State
University Press, 1964), pp. 312–53.
[26] William Thompson, "Illinois Constitutions" (Ph.D. diss., University of
Illinois, 1960), p. 233.
[27] Dunne, 2:424.
[28] William T. Hutchinson, *Lowden of Illinois: The Life of Frank O. Lowden,*
2 vols. (Chicago: University of Chicago Press, 1957), 1:86, 280.

limited to those things which properly constitute the fundamental law of the State, but have contained many matters which are properly the subject of legislation. . . . Legislation always depends upon existing conditions, and conditions change. A constitution which seeks to legislate will inevitably be outgrown. This is our situation to-day. Therefore, I strongly urge prompt adoption by the General Assembly of a resolution calling for a constitutional convention.

Lowden also included a plea for the short ballot, saying that "responsibility must be concentrated so that the people may know who is to blame if that responsibility is not met."[29] Eight days later, Senator Edward C. Curtis, who had introduced resolutions providing for a public vote on the question of calling a convention in every legislative session since 1909, introduced his resolution for the fifth time. It was adopted by the Senate on January 24, and by the House on March 14, 1917.[30]

In April 1918 George E. Cole, chairman of the Constitutional Convention Advisory Committee of the Citizens' Association of Chicago, called a meeting of those desiring a convention. The meeting was held in Governor Lowden's office in Springfield. A nonpartisan state organization — the Constitutional Convention Campaign Committee — was formed to conduct a campaign.[31] Educational material was prepared, including the pamphlet *Why Illinois Needs a New Constitution*. The pamphlet listed major groups favoring a convention call, including most of the state's leading newspapers, the Illinois State Bar Association, the Illinois State Bankers' Association, the Illinois State Farmers' Institute, the state meeting of the Corn Growers' and Stockmens' Organization, the Illinois Equal Suffrage Association, the Citizens' Association of Chicago, the Chicago Civic Federation, and the Chicago Association of Commerce.

The pamphlet also assured voters that a constitutional convention would not disrupt the existing system of government and law in the state. On the other hand, it pointed out, the state needed "preparation for peace." Now that the war was coming to an end, the live-

[29] Illinois, House, *Journal,* 1917, pp. 66–67.
[30] Illinois, Senate, *Journal,* 1917, p. 274; Illinois, House, *Journal,* 1917, p. 358.
[31] Carter, "Unofficial Steps," pp. 64–65.

liest kind of industrial, agricultural, and social development was expected. If the state were to keep pace with the times, restrictions of a bygone period had to be eliminated by the adoption of a new constitution.[32]

With the support of leading state groups and a well organized campaign, the convention question was approved by 562,012 votes, a majority of the 975,545 voting in the election on November 5, 1918.[33]

ELECTION OF DELEGATES

The voters had been urged to prepare for peace by calling a convention which would debate the fundamentals of state government, remove antiquated restrictions, and help the state effect changes expected in the "better world" which would come out of the horror of war. War experience could bring about such a state constitutional convention. The Massachusetts constitutional convention of 1919–20 has been called the "most searching political attempt made in Massachusetts to deal with fundamental problems." Nebraska's constitutional convention during the same years brought about moderate reforms, including a liberalized amendment procedure and revenue reform.[34] However, for a number of reasons the constitutional convention held in Illinois would take an opposite direction.

The way in which delegates were chosen deeply affected the nature of the Illinois constitutional convention of 1920–22. In 1919, the General Assembly passed an enabling act ordering a constitutional convention to assemble on January 6, 1920. Following instructions given in the constitution of 1870, two delegates were to be elected from each senatorial district, for a total of 102 delegates.[35] According to the 1870 constitution, delegates were to be elected "in the same manner, at the same places, and in the same districts" as

[32] Constitutional Convention Campaign Committee of Illinois, *Why Illinois Needs a New Constitution* (Springfield, 1918).

[33] A total of 162,206 votes was cast against the convention call. Not one Illinois county returned a vote against calling a convention. Cook County was the county most in favor of the convention call, producing a majority of 63,522½ votes. *Delegates' Manual,* pp. 67–68.

[34] J. A. Hague, "Massachusetts Constitutional Convention, 1917–19," *New England Quarterly* 27 (1919):149; Addison E. Sheldon, "Nebraska Constitutional Convention of 1919–20," *American Political Science Review* 15 (1921): 391–97.

[35] The enabling legislation is found in *Delegates' Manual,* pp. 71–74.

state senators. However, in 1870, senatorial candidates were chosen in party conventions, while in 1919 they were chosen in direct primaries.

The direct primary was a progressive innovation which sought to give the public more choice in selecting its candidates, and to avoid the selection of candidates by party committees in smoke-filled rooms. The direct primary had been bitterly fought for in Illinois; the state supreme court had overturned primary acts in 1905, 1906, and 1908 before the primary system was accepted in 1910.[36] Therefore, it is not surprising that committees of distinguished lawyers set up by the Constitutional Convention Campaign Committee and the Citizens' Association of Chicago expressed opinions that candidates for membership in the constitutional convention should first be nominated in direct primaries. On January 28, 1919, Attorney General Edward J. Brundage rendered his legal opinion that convention delegates had to be nominated in primary elections.[37] The enabling legislation of June 1919 therefore provided for primary election of nominees in September and the regular election of delegates on November 4, 1919.

Reliance on the direct primary inevitably introduced the element of partisanship into the process of delegate selection. Although Socialist party candidates entered the primaries in forty-two districts and were joined in the ensuing election by a handful of Labor party candidates,[38] delegate selection became primarily a concern of the Republican and Democratic parties. Furthermore, the primaries prevented any bipartisan delegations from being presented to the voters, as had been the case in 1848 and 1870.

The November 4 vote for delegates produced eighty-five Republicans and seventeen Democrats. This mirrored the current state and national trend toward the Republican party,[39] and reflected the fact that Republicans were in the forefront of agitation for constitutional reform, but it had unfortunate effects on the character of the con-

[36] Pease, *The Story of Illinois,* p. 223.
[37] Peter A. Tomei, "How Not to Hold a Constitutional Convention," *Chicago Bar Record* 49 (February 1968):182.
[38] *Delegates' Manual,* pp. 79–89.
[39] In 1920 Illinois chose Republican Harding for President by a vote of almost three to one, 1,420,480 to 534,395. During the twenties Republicans almost completely dominated state offices. Pease, *The Story of Illinois,* pp. 240–41.

vention and its chances for successful constitutional revision. Other constitutional conventions in Illinois had obtained public approval for their work only when the party membership of the convention had been almost evenly divided, and the resulting constitution had been a product of compromise between the two major parties. On the other hand, partisanship had been a major cause for the defeat of the 1862 constitution.

Another problem in delegate selection was the underrepresentation of Cook County resulting from the legislative failure to reapportion the state in 1911. Under the 1901 apportionment, Cook County was allotted nineteen senatorial districts, or thirty-eight convention delegates, while apportionment under actual population figures in 1919 would have given it forty-eight convention delegates.[40] Chicagoans, who had worked hardest for constitutional change, would have to depend on rural delegates and downstate urban delegates to sacrifice their own interests if an equitable reapportionment measure were to be passed.

By occupation and social status the delegates were hardly representative of a cross section of the Illinois population. Eighty percent of the total convention membership was accounted for by lawyers, businessmen, and doctors. The trend toward numerical dominance by the legal profession continued. The number of lawyers had increased in each convention. In 1920, fifty-six members named law as their main occupation, and many others were trained in law. Thirteen delegates represented agricultural interests, and there was only one union official, one union attorney, and no representative of the academic community.[41] Despite the impact of war on Illinois, only four convention members had served in the war while thirteen more had been active in local and state civil defense. The average age of convention members was slightly over fifty-one years.[42]

Many delegates had previously held public office; among them was Senator Curtis, who had labored so long for the calling of a convention. The delegates also included nine former members of

[40] Urban A. Lavery, "Status of the Illinois Constitutional Convention," *Illinois Law Review* 16 (1921–22):201.

[41] *Delegates' Manual*, pp. 111–15. A profile of each delegate to the convention is found on pp. 150–250.

[42] The youngest member was S. E. Pincus, 38; the oldest was ex-Governor Joseph Fifer, 79. Ibid., pp. 150–250.

the General Assembly, eight former judges, and seven former city mayors, as well as various other former officeholders. As in other Illinois constitutional conventions, several delegates were members of the current General Assembly, including the Speaker of the House, David E. Shanahan.[43]

The native origins of convention delegates reflected some of the great population changes in the state in the fifty years since the last constitutional convention. Whereas in 1870 only a small percentage of delegates were Illinois natives, in 1920 68 of the 102 members were born in Illinois, showing that Illinois was no longer a frontier state nor a stopping point in the movement of the population from East to West. Of the other delegates, only 8 came from the eastern or southern states; 12 were born in states bordering Illinois. The 9 foreign-born delegates' origins gave an indication of the most recent immigrations to Chicago and to Illinois. While in 1870 all the foreign-born delegates were from the British Isles, the 1920–22 convention included natives of Italy, Bohemia, Norway, and Germany, as well as Ireland, Scotland, and Canada. Chicago's black population, which in 1920 totalled over 100,000 and constituted 4 percent of the city's population, elected 2 prominent leaders of the black community as convention delegates.[44]

The Legislative Reference Bureau attempted to prepare the convention members for an informed consideration of the fundamental issues involved in constitutional revision and Illinois state government. As directed by the General Assembly in June of 1919, the bureau furnished the delegates with copies of earlier Illinois constitutions and their history, an annotated edition of the 1870 constitu-

---

[43] Other General Assembly members included Senator Curtis, Senator Henry M. Dunlap of Savoy, Senator Morton D. Hull, and Representatives Wm. M. Scanlan and Wm. H. Cruden. The question had arisen of the legality of electing members of the General Assembly to the convention, in view of constitutional restrictions against holding concurrent lucrative state offices (Art. IV, sec. 3), and Attorney General Brundage had indeed ruled that convention members would have to "vacate" their seats in the General Assembly. This ruling was disregarded by all but Senator Hull, who did resign his seat. During the 1920 election, four delegates were reelected to the General Assembly, and five additional convention members were elected to a second public office, two to the state Senate and three to the U.S. House of Representatives. None of these resigned from membership in the convention.

[44] U.S., Bureau of the Census, *Fourteenth Census*, 1920; Allan H. Spear, *Black Chicago: The Making of a Negro Ghetto, 1890–1920* (Chicago: University of Chicago Press, 1967), pp. 61, 64.

tion, fifteen bulletins surveying the operation of governmental institutions under the 1870 constitution, as well as information on other
state constitutions and constitutional problems likely to present themselves to the convention.[45] Unfortunately, the bureau's work had to
be done in the six months before the convention began, and most
of the materials did not reach the delegates until the eve of the convention, allowing little time for study.

The convention's timing, as well as its composition, influenced the
deliberations. The political machinery for a convention was put in
gear in 1916 by groups which had a specific idea of what they
wanted from state government. The delegates, however, did not
convene until 1920 in a very different postwar atmosphere. Chicago
and downstate business and professional leaders, once progressive
reformers, were now divided on such issues as the initiative and referendum, uncertain about the direction of state government, and
fearful of the specter of radical change.

THE FIFTH CONSTITUTIONAL CONVENTION

On January 6, 1920, the convention members assembled at the Hall
of the House of Representatives in the state capitol building in
Springfield where the convention was called to order by Governor
Lowden. The Republican majority decided to organize the convention by caucus, and it met with Governor Lowden on the morning
of January 6 to choose officers. This was an ominous note; in 1862
Democrats had organized the convention before it had even assembled, and the result was partisan convention proceedings and a
partisan constitution rejected by the voters. The 1848 and 1870 conventions had elected their officers through compromises between the
two major parties.

The convention unanimously selected as president Charles E.
Woodward of La Salle County, Governor Lowden's close friend and
draftsman of the famed Civil Administrative Code of Illinois.[46]
Woodward was elected unanimously in recognition of his outstand-
ing ability and in the interests of harmony; however, the Repub-

[45] Illinois, Legislative Reference Bureau, *General Statement of Work of Legislative Reference Bureau* (Springfield, 1919), pp. 5–7.
[46] *Delegates' Manual*, p. 146.

lican's choice for secretary, Bert McCann, was opposed by the Democrats, who wished to organize the convention on a bipartisan basis as in 1870, with a Republican for president, a Democrat for secretary, and so on. In presenting the minority candidate for secretary, Franklin Dove of Shelby County made the following argument for bipartisan organization:

> Deliberative bodies and especially a Constitutional Convention should be run and operated less along political lines than any other body. There may be some excuse, gentlemen, for a legislative body being conducted along party lines. They may have a definite program which they wish to enact into law, but the very purpose of a Constitutional Convention is to . . . safeguard the rights of the minority from the enforced will of a majority.

> There is no better time than here and now to see to it that this Convention is not organized along party and political lines. I think I am safe in saying that I voice the sentiment of every delegate here that our principal duty is to formulate a document which will have the support of this State. To that end it is necessary that we have the confidence of all parties. The constitutional rights of a Democrat, a Republican, a Prohibitionist, a Socialist and a Progressive are all the same.[47]

Despite this argument, Republicans elected McCann on a straight party vote, 82 to 17. The intent was clear; the constitutional convention was to operate on a party basis. Organization by party continued in committee assignments, with Democrats being given only three of the twenty-five committee chairmanships.[48]

The delegates took the oath of office without debate.[49] In this case, the intention of the 1870 convention to avoid controversy by specifying the oath to be taken was successful. The convention appointed a committee to establish rules and procedure and then adjourned for eight days to await the committee's report.[50]

---

[47] *Proceedings of the Constitutional Convention of the State of Illinois Convened January 6, 1920*, 5 vols. (Springfield, 1920–22), 1:37–38.

[48] *Delegates' Manual*, pp. 129–31.

[49] *Proceedings of the Convention* (1920–22), 1:41.

[50] This report has been criticized for some of its provisions, such as the lack of time limitations on debate, which contributed to both the acrimony of the convention and its length. Another criticism came on committee assignments. Although there were 102 members, each received several committee assignments, which seriously impeded committee work. *Delegates' Manual*, pp. 117–28, 131–38.

This was only the first of a number of adjournments and recesses which prolonged the duration of the convention to two years and nine months, the longest by far in Illinois constitution making.[51] Several factors contributed to the unusual length of the convention. Poor organization was one cause. Delegates held sessions only two or three days a week, and at first committees rarely met. Members demanded summer vacations because of the heat. The convention recessed for the legislative session in 1921, as apparently no one suggested moving the convention site from the capitol building for the duration. The convention, officially in session for almost three years, spent only 140 days in actual convention work.[52]

Absenteeism became a major problem. The meager $2,000 salary provided for convention delegates had attracted men who thought of their convention duties as a public service, but as the convention dragged on, most of them had to return to making a living. The convention usually conducted business with barely a quorum present. Attendance improved after those delegates who did attend regularly passed a measure on April 25, 1922, to have the absent delegates brought to the convention under physical custody of the sergeant-at-arms.[53] By this time, however, the public had lost whatever interest and confidence it had had in the convention's work.

The Committee on Phraseology and Style also contributed to the length of the convention by requesting recesses in order to draft a "noble Document." The committee attempted to eliminate the vagueness, ambiguity, and archaic phraseology of the 1870 constitution by completely revising its text.[54] This resulted in delays in finishing the work of the convention.

Another important reason underlying the many recesses in the convention's work was the bitter schism between Cook County and other Illinois delegates. The convention adjourned when neither side

[51] The convention assembled again on January 14, recessed from July 7 to September 21, immediately recessed again until November 8 and again on December 8. The convention did not reconvene until January 1922, recessing again for six-week periods in the spring of 1922 and for two and one-half months in the summer. The convention finally adjourned on September 12, 1922. Tomei, p. 189.

[52] Tomei, p. 186.

[53] *Proceedings of the Convention* (1920–22), 4:3735.

[54] *Comment of Committee on Phraseology and Style on Second Revised Draft of the Constitution of Illinois* (Springfield, 1922), p. 6.

could agree or communicate with the other, especially on matters of legislative apportionment and the question of the initiative and referendum.

The initiative and referendum had been one of the most popular progressive attempts to give the public more control over the legislative process. By 1915 twenty-one states had adopted it in some form. Illinois voters also had advocated its adoption in advisory referenda in 1902 and 1910,[55] and in a similar advisory referenda when choosing convention delegates in November 1919. However, the initiative and referendum issue divided parties and reform groups on a Cook County-downstate basis.[56] Groups outside Cook County, spearheaded by agricultural leaders, argued that the initiative and referendum gave weight to public interests purely on a majority rule basis. In Illinois this would mean Chicago interests would dominate and would give no consideration to the special needs of minority occupational groups such as farmers.[57] Advocates of the initiative and referendum included Duncan McDonald, president of the Illinois Federation of Labor, and ex-Governor Dunne. Dunne argued that the legislature was not responsive to the people, but to pressure groups. In testifying before the convention, he described how "contaminating lobbies, financed by corporate influence, have infested legislative halls and the hotels where legislators live, and have influenced the legislators by sinister arguments delivered in closets and bathrooms, behind closed doors." To keep this hold on the legislature, Dunne warned, "all the reactionary and capitalistic influence of the State" opposed the initiative and referendum.[58]

Despite such arguments, however, the convention voted 52 to 20 not to include a provision for the initiative, referendum, and recall in the constitution.[59] Some Chicago delegates were so incensed at this action, in view of the vote in the pre-convention referendum, that M. A. Michaelson immediately moved that the convention adjourn

[55] Bogart and Mathews, p. 376.

[56] In the 1919 advisory referenda, Cook County tabulated 148,646 for submission of the initiative and referendum question and 76,267 against. Other counties voted 108,994 for and 133,081 against. Earl T. Hanson, "The Chicago-Downstate Problem as Shown by the Illinois Constitutional Convention of 1920–1922" (master's thesis, University of Illinois, 1939), p. 78.

[57] *Proceedings of the Convention* (1920–22), 1:714–81.

[58] Ibid., 1:239–43.

[59] Ibid., 3:2522.

sine die, claiming that "this convention had failed in its purpose." Eight delegates voted with him in favor of adjournment.[60] The following day the *Chicago Herald and Examiner* wrote that "it is generally conceded in Springfield that when the convention buried the I and R it ended all hope for the new constitution, indelibly okayed by the interests."[61] After the initial uproar subsided, the initiative and referendum controversy continued to plague the proceedings. H. I. Green, Champaign County attorney and prominent convention delegate, claimed that one of the causes for frequent adjournments was the insistent demand for its resurrection. Adjournments came partly for the purpose of letting this demand subside. The initiative and referendum question also contributed to the decision to submit the document to the voters as a whole. Separate submission of other controversial articles, while ignoring the I and R, would have been embarrassing in view of the pre-convention referendum.[62]

Seventy of the convention members met for the last time on September 12, 1922, when they completed their business, heard the address to the people written for publication with the constitution, and signed the document. The delegates authorized the printing of one million copies of the annotated constitution together with the address to the people, and the convention adjourned.

PROPOSED CONSTITUTION OF 1922

The proposed constitution differed sharply in language and organization from that of 1870; in fact, when the two constitutions were published together by the Bureau of Public Efficiency in order to note the differences between them, it was found impossible to print them side by side, and explanations and cross references had to be used to compare the two.[63] The proposed constitution of 1922 retained the preamble of other Illinois constitutions, but dropped the article on boundaries, reasoning that state boundaries were fixed by act of Congress and not determined by the state. The bill of rights

[60] Ibid.
[61] *Chicago Herald and Examiner,* November 24, 1920. The *Herald* had been one of the foremost advocates of the initiative and referendum.
[62] Personal interview with H. I. Green in Hanson, p. 82.
[63] Chicago Bureau of Public Efficiency, *The Proposed New Constitution for Illinois* (Chicago, 1922) pp. 7–8.

contained most of the provisions of the 1870 constitution, though it was extensively rewritten to remove archaic and unnecessary phrases. Section 5 would have permitted the waiving of a jury trial in all but capital cases, expanding this practice somewhat over the 1870 provision as interpreted by the courts. Section 5 also permitted women to serve as jurors for the first time.

The argument in the 1869–70 convention over Bible reading in the public schools was renewed in 1920. The state supreme court had held that Article II, section 3 of the 1870 constitution, guaranteeing religious freedom, prohibited Bible reading in the schools, and many members wanted to include in the new constitution express permission for Bible reading.[64] The debate repeated arguments on both sides similar to those in the 1870 convention; in fact, statements of Joseph Medill, William H. Underwood, and others in the convention of 1870 on the same subject were quoted in the debate. Organized opponents of Bible reading in the schools included Lutherans, Catholics, and Jews. The Lutherans feared it would be an opening wedge towards greater control of religion by the state. Catholics and Jews believed the Bible used for reading would be the King James version, and would therefore be an imposition of alien beliefs upon their children. Proponents quoted Benjamin Franklin, Thomas Jefferson, Abraham Lincoln, and George Washington and appealed to their colleagues to "keep God in American government." The best-received speech, by Rodney H. Brandon of Kane County, asserted that Bible reading in the schools "gives our people . . . the chance to know that their children each day, when the work is begun, are once more impressed with the principle that every organized human effort should be begun by a recognition of man's dependence upon Deity." The convention voted, 45 to 16, to include a phrase in the third section of the bill of rights providing that "the reading of selections from any version of the Old and New Testaments in the public schools without comment shall never be held to be in conflict with this constitution."[65]

Another addition to the bill of rights stated that "laws shall be applicable alike to all citizens without regard to race or color." Black

[64] Illinois, Legislative Reference Bureau, *Constitution of the State of Illinois, Annotated* (Springfield, 1919), p. 29.
[65] *Proceedings of the Convention* (1920–22), 4:3566–611.

delegate Edward H. Morris, a successful corporation lawyer and attorney for Cook County and an active worker for equal rights movements, fought vigorously for a strong guarantee of civil rights. He was supported by a majority of the convention members present, but many delegates indicated during debate that their sentiments had not progressed very far from the thinking of 1862, when Illinois voters denied blacks the rights of citizenship. Delegate Morris and his colleague, the Reverend Archibald Carey, another powerful figure in political and social concerns in the Chicago black community, asserted pride in their race and pointed to black accomplishments during the Civil War, Spanish-American War, and World War I.[66] The attack against them and their position by some convention members centered almost exclusively on the question of racial intermarriage, an issue which the black delegates felt was irrelevant to the question of civil rights in the constitution:

> Mr. McEwen (Cook). Do you think it would be a good thing for the people of this country if the races were permitted to intermingle and assemble?
>
> Mr. Morris (Cook). I think it would be a good thing for this country if we as lawmakers attended to our own business and let the individuals attend to theirs, along those lines.[67]

Members continued to voice their fears about racial intermarriage, but the Reverend Mr. Carey delivered what many felt to be the final word on the subject of the purity of the races:

> If there came, sir, any mixture in my blood, it was due to crime on the part of the men of your race when my great grandmother was a slave, and helpless, and couldn't defend herself nor her virtue. (Applause)[68]

The provision for equal administration of the law without regard to race or color passed, 58 to 5 — but only after some members were assured by their colleagues that it would not interfere with the General Assembly's future right to pass laws forbidding intermarriage between races.[69]

[66] Ibid., 2:1975–78; 4:3700–702.
[67] Ibid., 2:1979.
[68] Ibid., 4:3700.
[69] Ibid., 4:4059.

The most bitter controversy in the legislative article — some felt in the whole constitution — was the question of reapportionment of the legislature. The fears of Chicagoans — that constitutional revision would mean an attempt to keep them a permanent minority in the state legislature — were justified. The majority report on the question, signed by downstate members of the Committee on the Legislative Department, provided for restriction of Cook County in both houses of the General Assembly. Cook County would receive nineteen of the fifty-one senatorial districts, and in the House of Representatives each county would be a unit of representation with one representative, plus one additional representative for each 50,000 inhabitants. After the first apportionment, no county could have its representation reduced if it lost population. A minority report, signed by Cook County members of the committee, both Republicans and Democrats, placed no restrictions on the representation of Cook County in either house of the legislature. A third report was submitted by a Democratic delegate, and complained that neither of the other two plans provided for cumulative voting.[70]

On June 17, 1920, the convention accepted in principle the majority report provisions. The state was to be divided into 57 senatorial districts, with Cook County containing 19 and other counties 38 districts. There were to be 153 representative districts, with no county allowed to have more than seventy-six representatives. Thus, Cook County representation was to be limited in both houses. This plan was adopted by a vote of 43 to 19, being opposed by sixteen Cook County and three downstate delegates.[71]

News of the apportionment plan created an uproar, and contributed greatly to the difficulties of the convention, as Chicago delegates refused to accept the majority decision, and downstate members refused to compromise. Finally, however, an agreement was worked out on February 7, 1922, in which Cook County would not be limited in representation in the House, but would be limited to one-third of the Senate membership.[72] This compromise came

[70] *Journal of the Constitutional Convention, 1920–1922, of the State of Illinois* (Springfield, 1922), p. 199–201. Cumulative voting, at that time supported mainly by the Democratic Party, was not included in the final reapportionment plan adopted by the convention.

[71] Ibid., p. 210.

[72] Ibid., pp. 491–93.

too late for many Chicagoans, who had become prejudiced against the convention in the long months after its first apportionment decision. Others denounced the compromise and held out for true proportional representation in both houses.

The Chicago-downstate fight over representation continued in the judicial article. In the 1870 constitution, Cook, Will, Lake, Kankakee, and Du Page counties had been designated as one of the seven supreme court districts, each of which elected one justice. In the proposed constitution, the same districts were preserved, but the number of justices was to be increased to nine. The district including Cook County was to elect three judges, although only two of them could be elected from Cook.[73] This provision gave more judicial representation to the Cook County areas than had the 1870 constitution, but it still clearly underrepresented the most populous areas. The district including Cook, Will, Lake, Kankakee, and Du Page counties, containing a majority of the state's population, was permanently restricted to one-third of the supreme court positions.

Another controversial section of the judicial article would have given the supreme court original jurisdiction over cases relating to revenue, in quo warranto, mandamus, habeus corpus, prohibition, and "other cases involving questions of great public importance." The supreme court was also given the power to "prescribe rules of pleading, practice and procedure in all courts," to appoint and remove appellate court judges, and assign circuit court justices and appoint their assistants. This section was considered a praiseworthy attempt to give some centralized direction to Illinois's court system, but possibly dangerous because of the extraordinary powers which might accrue to the supreme court through future interpretations of the measure.

The suffrage article provoked little debate in the convention. Woman suffrage had failed in 1870, but in 1920 the delegates seemingly accepted its inevitability. The only question was whether striking out the word "male" in the article would be a sufficient guaran-

[73] Proposed constitution of 1922, Art. V, sec. 87, 88. This document is found in the proceedings and the journal of the 1920–22 convention, and in *The Proposed New Constitution of Illinois, 1922, with Explanatory Notes and Address to the People* (Springfield, 1922).

tee of the vote to women.[74] Black suffrage was not debated again, except by implication. One delegate proposed withholding suffrage from those "who cannot read and write the English language." George F. Lohman of Cook County predicted that if this restriction were included, it would lead to literacy tests and the disenfranchisement of many black voters, as had similar provisions in other states. The provision was subsequently voted down.[75]

The unfair and regressive nature of state taxation was a major factor in demands for the constitutional convention in 1920, but the proposed constitution's revenue provisions pleased no one. The revenue article provided that the general property tax would remain, but authorized the legislature to provide a substitute flat rate tax on incomes from intangible personal property. The legislature could also levy a general tax on all net incomes.[76] The income tax proposition was a controversial but courageous method of attacking the state's revenue problems. However, the delegates' concern for business interests and fear of future public actions led them to place detailed constitutional restrictions on the tax. The income tax could be graduated, but the highest rate could never exceed three times the lowest rate. Exemptions could be granted to low-income families, but these exemptions could never exceed "one thousand dollars to the head of a family plus two hundred dollars for each dependent child under the age of sixteen years," or five hundred dollars for a single person.

One of the major reasons Chicagoans had supported a constitutional convention was the desire for greater home rule for the city. The local government article of the proposed constitution devoted sixteen sections to specifying home rule for Chicago, which did grant many powers to the city, but the article was limited by a clause which stated that "the city, however, may impose taxes and borrow

[74] *Proceedings of the Convention* (1920–22), 1:967–77. The nineteenth amendment to the U.S. Constitution went into effect on August 26, 1920, while the convention was in official session.

[75] Ibid., 1:996–99.

[76] The income tax, "if levied, would be in addition to other taxes authorized, but in order to avoid double taxation, the General Assembly may permit deductions to compensate for other taxes paid on the property (or income therefrom) from which the income taxed under the general income tax is derived." Chicago Bureau of Public Efficiency, *Shall the Proposed New Constitution Be Adopted? Vote Yes* (Chicago, 1922), p. 12.

money only as authorized by the general assembly or by this article."
This failed to satisfy Chicago's demands.

A later critic said of the 1920–22 convention that "it proceeded
as if it were framing a constitution for an abstract Utopia of its own
creation, instead of the state of Illinois with living people and rather
concrete and easily ascertainable political opinions."[77] Nowhere was
this harsh judgment more clearly upheld than in the provisions made
in the convention for future amendments to the new document.
Despite the trouble experienced in amending the 1870 constitution
and the extreme efforts required to obtain enough votes to call a
convention in 1920, the delegates ignored the opportunity to write
a more flexible amending process into the proposed constitution.
The new document retained the same requirements for calling a new
convention, including the requirement that a convention call be
approved by a majority of all those voting at an election. Despite
controversies before the 1920 convention which had to be settled by
rulings by the attorney general, the provisions for choosing delegates
to a convention were unchanged. As in 1920, the members would
be chosen from senate districts. Cook County, allotted one-third of
these districts in the legislative article, was given seven extra convention seats. Even with this modification Cook County was assured
of minority status in a future convention, an additional reason for
Chicago's opposition to the document.

Amendments still had to be approved by two-thirds vote in both
houses of the General Assembly. The number of electors needed to
approve amendments was reduced from a majority of all those
voting in the election to a majority of those voting for members of
the House of Representatives. The General Assembly was limited to
proposing amendments to not more than two articles of the constitution at the same session, "nor to the same section oftener than once
in four years."

The convention delegates held little debate on the subject of making the calling of a convention or the amending of the constitution
easier to accomplish. Evidently most agreed with ex-Governor Fifer
when he said that "we ought to make it [the constitution] so that it

[77] Henry P. Chandler, "Thoughts on Constitution-Making Suggested by the
Experience of Illinois," *University of Pennsylvania Law Review* 71 (1923):
222.

cannot be changed lightly and easily. We want it so secure that when we go home after our adjournment and the people adopt it, we can go about our usual vocations with the assurance that no great harm can come to us or the rest of our fellow citizens by hasty and inconsiderate legislation."[78]

The schedule of the proposed constitution provided for its submission to the voters at a special election on Tuesday, December 12, 1922. The decision to submit it as a whole dampened its chances of adoption. Many groups were opposed to certain provisions and might have supported the document if allowed to vote separately on controversial issues. As it was, opposing groups, while differing among themselves, were united in their opposition. Given the chance either to accept the constitution with objectionable provisions or to reject it, most chose to reject it.

Voter Rejection of the Constitution

In the three-month interval between the convention's adjournment and the special election, both proponents and opponents of the document organized public opinion campaigns. The convention itself published a pamphlet containing the text of the new constitution along with an address praising its strong points, which had been written by the convention's Committee on Submission and Address. The voters were requested "not to approach [the document] with the mind to compare it with his ideal, for this is to condemn it in advance. . . . The real and only question presented to the people of Illinois is: Is this proposed new Constitution, framed by your representatives, better than the Constitution under which you now live?" To assist the voter in answering this question, each section of the constitution was accompanied by notes which indicated the changes, if any, from the 1870 constitution.[79]

A state committee organized to promote adoption of the new constitution was headed by Chief State Supreme Court Justice Orrin N. Carter, with former Governor Lowden, former Governor Charles S. Deneen, U.S. Senator William B. McKinley, and former U.S. Senator Lawrence Y. Sherman as honorary vice-presidents.

---

[78] *Proceedings of the Convention* (1920–22), 5:4381.
[79] *The Proposed New Constitution of Illinois, with Explanatory Notes and Address to the People*, p. 5.

Members of the committee from Cook County included leading railroad and utility lawyers, a fact which probably hurt the constitution's chances, since opponents charged that it had been written mainly for corporation interests.[80] County committees were organized to provide speakers and furnish literature promoting the advantages of the new constitution.[81] Also active in advocating the constitution's adoption was the Chicago Bureau of Public Efficiency, which prepared both a straightforward publication entitled *The Proposed New Constitution for Illinois,* containing the text of the proposed document and the text of the old with extensive explanatory comments and cross references, and a more argumentative pamphlet entitled *Shall the Proposed New Constitution be Adopted? Vote Yes.*

On November 22, 1922, opponents organized the People's Protective League with Harold L. Ickes as president and former Governor Dunne and attorney Clarence Darrow among its members. The members of the league waged an active campaign, preparing and distributing pamphlets and making public statements and speeches against the adoption of the constitution.[82]

Various newspapers, civic organizations, and political factions in the state began to take sides on the question. Chicago newspapers, which had vigorously advocated a convention four years before, were almost unanimously opposed to the convention's finished product. The *Tribune* stated editorially:

> Vote no on the question of adopting the proposed constitution. If it were accepted the people of this state would write into their fundamental law an unjust and unAmerican doctrine of inequality in political rights. This unjust doctrine would deprive Cook County of its full representation in the state senate and it would limit Chicago to two of the nine Supreme Court judges.

The *Daily Journal* and the *Herald and Examiner* also opposed the constitution, while the *Evening Post* supported it.[83]

[80] *Chicago Herald and Examiner,* November 18, 1922.

[81] *Urbana Daily Courier,* November 22, 1922. This and the following newspaper citations are taken from clippings compiled by Jane Tufford, Illinois Historical Survey, Urbana.

[82] *Chicago Herald and Examiner,* November 24, 1922; Dunne, pp. 429–30.

[83] *Chicago Tribune,* December 10, 1922; *Chicago Evening Post,* December 11, 1922.

Springfield's two papers disagreed on the issue of adopting the constitution. The Republican *State Journal* supported it luke-warmly, saying that the new document "was superior to the present constitution, all things considered, and more responsive to the modern demands of the state and the needs of its people." The Democratic *State Register,* on the other hand, opposed it because the new constitution "was framed subtly in the interest of special interests," and besides, it would raise taxes. According to the *Urbana Daily Courier,* downstate newspapers on the whole showed a favorable attitude towards the constitution because of improvements in the tax system, judicial reform, and above all, the permanent limitation of Chicago's representation in the state senate.[84]

Political opposition to the proposed constitution grew. The Democratic central committee of Cook County went on record as opposing the constitution by a vote of 43 to 3, while Anton J. Cermak, Democratic president of the Cook County Board of Commissioners, urged the voters to "snow it under." Republicans were split on the issue. Since 1918 the Republican party in Illinois had been bitterly divided into two factions, one led by former Governor Lowden and the other by Governor Len Small and Chicago Mayor William (Big Bill) Thompson. Lowden had supported the convention's efforts from the beginning; Thompson and Small now opposed it. Small especially criticized the revenue article, arguing that "instead of equalizing taxation, the revenue sections of the document offered the voters are so framed as to relieve and favor the very rich and impose unequal and burdensome taxation upon the poor man, the wage-earner and the person of moderate means." The governor also criticized the submission of the document as a whole instead of by sections.[85]

Although the Illinois State Federation of Labor opposed the constitution through fear of a "judicial dictatorship," judges themselves were divided on its merits. The supreme court split; three of the seven judges opposed the constitution because it would give the court undesirable powers and drag the supreme court into politics. Twenty-five judges of the circuit and superior courts of Cook

[84] *Illinois State Journal,* December 12, 1922; *Illinois State Register,* December 11, 1922; *Urbana Daily Courier,* December 11, 1922.

[85] *Chicago Tribune,* December 10, 11, 1922.

County signed a "round robin" which urged the defeat of the proposed basic law. Opponents' claims that it was a lawyer's and not a people's constitution were reinforced by its support from the legal profession. The *Illinois Law Review* asked for the opinions of twenty-nine prominent attorneys throughout Illinois, and twenty-seven favored adoption of the constitution, as did the Chicago Bar Association.[86]

Chicago members of the Illinois State Teachers' Association adopted resolutions condemning the work of the convention, the executive committee of the World's War Veterans denounced the proposed document by calling it "the most reactionary measure ever attempted to be foisted on a free and independent people," and the Rotary Club, at first expected to endorse the new constitution, decided not to take an official stand.[87]

The vote on the issue on December 12, 1922, was extremely heavy, totaling over a million votes. The constitution was emphatically rejected, 921,398 votes against and 185,298 for. Voters outside Cook County rejected the constitution by more than two to one while Cook County returned a negative vote of nearly twenty to one.[88] The *Chicago Herald and Examiner* said, "There is no record in the history of American politics that equals this for an uprising of the people at the ballot box on a local issue." The *New York Times* reported that "the majority is incredible."[89]

Blame for the crushing defeat of the proposed 1922 constitution has been laid to many factors, primarily the partisanship of the convention, the submission of the document as a whole, the loss of popular interest because of the length of the convention, the attempt to rewrite the entire constitution, and the lack of liberal amending procedures. The support of almost every major faction and group in the state was necessary to approve constitutions in 1848 and 1870. On the other hand, the 1862 constitution was rejected mainly because the convention had alienated a major group — the Republican party. The 1920–22 convention members managed not only to

[86] Ibid., December 11; *Chicago Herald and Examiner,* November 3, 11, 1922.

[87] *Chicago Herald and Examiner,* November 19, 21, 22, 1922.

[88] The Cook County vote was 27,874 for and 541,206 against; outside Cook the vote was 157,424 for and 380,192 against. *Illinois Blue Book,* 1923–24, p. 791.

[89] December 13, 1922.

alienate some Republican party members, but also most of the Democrats, labor unions, teachers, judges, and many other groups in the state, including most Cook County residents. The convention of 1920–22, however, did perform several services: the background work prepared by the Legislative Reference Bureau remains, and a study of the 1920–22 convention made in 1969 examined "how not to hold a constitutional convention."[90]

CONVENTION REFERENDUM, 1934

After the convention method of changing the 1870 constitution failed in 1922, other attempts were made to change the constitution through the amendment process. However, as before, the requirement of a favorable vote by a majority of those voting at an election thwarted these efforts. Gateway amendments failed in 1924 and 1932, and revenue amendments failed in 1926 and 1930. All but one of these produced a strong favorable majority of those voting on the question, but 40 percent or more of Illinois voters voting in the election ignored the amendment propositions. In 1929, Governor Louis Emmerson supported the movement, adopted by the legislature, to return amendment questions to their original place on the left side of the official ballot feeling that the "little ballot" experiment had proved unsuccessful.[91] However, results were even worse under this experiment. While at least 70 percent of Illinois voters had participated in voting on amendment questions when they were on the "little ballot," in none of the constitutional proposals submitted from 1930 to 1950 did as many as half of the voters bother to mark that particular question on their ballot.[92]

As Illinois voters exhibited disinterest and passivity on constitutional amendment questions, grave defects in state government, at least partly attributable to judicial interpretations of the 1870 constitution, remained. Revenue provided the clearest example. In the Great Depression, the property tax as a reliable source of state rev-

[90] See Peter Tomei's article of this title written in the spring of 1968 before submission of another convention referendum to the voters in November of that year.
[91] Kenneth C. Sears, "Voting on Constitutional Conventions and Amendments," *University of Chicago Law Review* 2 (1935):612–18.
[92] Illinois Legislative Council, *Constitutional Revision*, p. 12.

enue collapsed. In 1932, the Illinois General Assembly enacted a graduated income tax. However, the Illinois Supreme Court in *Bachrach* v. *Nelson* ruled that the constitution allowed the General Assembly to tax "property, occupations, and franchises and privileges only." This narrow interpretation of the General Assembly's taxing power also ruled out a sales tax. However, the legislature circumvented this by framing the sales tax as an "occupation tax" which businesses automatically passed on to their customers. The sales tax in this unsatisfactory form became the primary source of state revenue after 1932.[93]

Another serious and divisive issue in any discussion of constitutional revision in Illinois is the matter of apportionment. The legislature was still represented according to the 1901 apportionment. Chicago in the 1930s continued to send nineteen senators and fifty-seven representatives to the legislature. Reapportionment according to the 1930 census would have given Cook County a majority representation of twenty-six senators and seventy-eight representatives. Population movements outside Chicago had also created "pocket boroughs" where voters were overrepresented, as well as other underrepresented areas.[94] The courts in Illinois continued to refuse to order the legislature to reapportion. In a number of decisions from 1926 to 1930 they refused "to enjoin salary payments to legislators for failure to redistrict," or to test legislators' rights to office under an outmoded apportionment act, or to adopt the view that an act of the legislature is invalid if passed by a body which is itself "invalidly" constituted because of failure to redistrict.[95] The federal courts also refused to act. An Illinois citizen sought to enjoin the collector of internal revenue from collecting federal income taxes on the grounds that failure to reapportion deprived Illinois of a republican form of government, but his contention was held to be without merit by the Circuit Court of Appeals, and in 1931 the

[93] JoDesha Lucas, "Legal Aspects of Revenue," in *Con-Con: Issues for the Illinois Constitutional Convention,* ed. Samuel K. Gove and Victoria Ranney (Urbana: University of Illinois Press, 1970), pp. 357–58.
[94] Elson, "Constitutional Revision," p. 17.
[95] *Fergus* v. *Marks,* 321 Ill. 510 (1926); *Fergus* v. *Kinney,* 333 Ill. 437 (1929); *People* v. *Blackwell,* 342 Ill. 223 (1930); *People* v. *Clardy,* 334 Ill. 160 (1929); Illinois Legislative Council, *Legislative Apportionment,* p. 5.

U.S. Supreme Court, on appeal, dismissed the suit for want of jurisdiction.[96]

With the reapportionment issue thus unresolved, and the failure again in 1932 of another Gateway proposal, new efforts were made to call a constitutional convention. The question was submitted to the voters at the general election November 6, 1934.

To assist in gathering support for this convention call, the Legislative Reference Bureau published a pamphlet which briefly summarized Illinois constitutional history to 1934 and included reasons why a constitutional convention was needed. The pamphlet listed problem areas in Illinois state government which demanded remedies, including an antiquated and inequitable taxing system, the apportionment situation, the lack of municipal home rule for Chicago and other cities, the overrepresentation of minority parties in the cumulative voting system, disproportionate and unfair judicial districts and other faults of the judicial system, the impracticable and unworkable double liability of bank stockholders, inefficient and wasteful county and local governments, and the restrictive and difficult amending process.[97]

The pamphlet also attempted to answer some of the arguments against a convention call in 1934. To the fear that a new constitution would overturn present judicial interpretations or necessitate the rewriting of a large part of the statutes, the pamphlet asserted that revision of the most objectionable provisions of the document would leave the great bulk of the constitution, and hence the fundamental law, unchanged. Another argument was that the disproportionate allotment of senate districts would mean, as in 1920, that a convention would represent a minority of the population. In reply proponents pointed out that this was actually a strong argument for a convention call, since the malapportionment in the General Assembly was evidently going to continue until a revision of the con-

[96] The petitioner in the federal cases, John W. Keogh, later argued before Circuit Judge John Prystalski of Chicago that the legislature was illegal. When the judge refused to listen, Keogh shot and killed the opposing lawyer and then shot at the judge because he felt "something drastic had to be done to awaken the people." Illinois Legislative Council, *Legislative Apportionment*, p. 5.

[97] Illinois, Legislative Reference Bureau, *The Constitution of Illinois* (Springfield, 1934), pp. 34–70.

stitution forced the legislature to act equitably and reapportion the state.[98]

One argument remained: to some it seemed unwise to call a convention in the unstable economic and political atmosphere of 1934. The *Chicago Tribune,* the most vocal opponent of a convention call, warned:

> No one knows what a new constitution may provide, but everyone knows that we are passing through a period of extraordinary emotional strain. The times are made to order the acceptance of political quackery and economic nostrums. Naziism, other forms of Fascism, and communism are spreading over the civilized world. They have already made inroads in our country. A constitutional convention meeting at this time may not be swept off its feet by mass hysterias, but the danger is great; it is avoidable and it should be avoided. . . .
>
> The proposal to hold a constitutional convention is a proposal to create new emotional strains at a time of great emotional excitement. It is a proposal to revive old animosities and create new ones. The convention would provide just such troubled waters as Communists and Fascists most desire. They could ask no better opportunity to destroy free government.[99]

Despite the fearful specter of radicalism raised by the *Tribune,* the 1934 convention call received a majority of the votes of those voting on the question, 691,021 in favor and 585,879 opposed. The referendum failed, however. Fifty-six and one-half percent of those voting in the election did not express an opinion on the question.[100] Public apathy and ignorance about constitutional reform, perhaps aided by the fear of radicalism and the dislike of spending money for a convention,[101] were the apparent causes for its defeat.

OTHER DEVELOPMENTS

After the failure of the 1934 convention call, attempts to amend the constitution continued without success. By 1946 four amend-

[98] Ibid., pp. 72–74.
[99] *Chicago Tribune,* August 7, 1934.
[100] Illinois Legislative Council, *Constitutional Revision,* p. 14.
[101] Kenneth C. Sears, "Constitutional Revision in Illinois," *Illinois Law Review* 33 (1938):10.

ment proposals had been submitted to the voters but none had received the majority necessary for approval. In 1938 the voters rejected an amendment to the banking provisions of Article XI which would have removed the double liability of state bank stockholders and permitted amendments to the general banking laws to be adopted by a two-thirds vote of each house of the General Assembly instead of the existing requirement of approval at a general election by a majority of those voting on the proposition. An amendment exempting the sale of food from the sales tax failed in 1942, followed in 1944 by the failure of an amendment allowing county sheriffs and treasurers to succeed themselves. In 1946 the fifth attempt to liberalize the amending process of the 1870 constitution was unsuccessful. The proposed Gateway amendment would have replaced the old provision that required approval by a majority of those voting in the election with a less stringent provision requiring approval by two-thirds of those voting on the constitutional question.[102]

By the late 1930s and 1940s nineteenth century state constitutions like that of Illinois were in great disrepute. Their superfluous provisions, restrictions, and antiquated and faulty legal terminology seemed to function mainly to impede needed progress and development. Constitutions were good "whipping boys" on which to fix the blame for the inadequacy and rigidity of state government and the states' loss of prestige and power during those decades. At the same time state governments were being eclipsed by Washington in a centralizing trend which assigned the federal government the primary role in coping with depression and war crises. Constitutional scholars questioned whether the states themselves had any viable function in American government, and whether they should even be preserved.[103] Others, however, continued their efforts to revamp state government, attacking the problem as usual through constitutional revision.[104] In Illinois a small group of constitutional scholars and political scientists kept the issue of constitutional revision alive.

[102] *Constitution of the State of Illinois* (1967), p. 10.
[103] Earl H. DeLong, "States' Rights and the State Executive," *Illinois Law Review* 33 (1938):42; Edward S. Corwin, "The Passing of Dual Federalism," *Virginia Law Review* 36 (1950):23.
[104] See, for example, Vernon A. O'Rourke and Douglas W. Campbell, *Constitution-Making in a Democracy: Theory and Practice in New York State* (Baltimore: The Johns Hopkins Press, 1943).

VI

Constitutional Developments
1946–1968

A renewed movement for revision of the Illinois Constitution of
1870 began in the mid-1940s under young and vigorous leadership.
After the fifth Gateway proposal failed to win voter approval in
1946, its proponents, including Walter Schaefer and Samuel W.
Witwer, led a small group of citizens to Springfield to urge the
calling of a constitutional convention. Their lack of success led to
the formation of the Committee on Constitutional Revision of the
Chicago Bar Association to organize a more thorough effort. Members of this committee, headed by Witwer, included Schaefer, Adlai
Stevenson II, Steven Mitchell, Otto Kerner, Walter Cummings, Jr.,
Barnet Hodius, and Wayland Cedarquist. The committee comprised
a young, able, ambitious and idealistic elite — the spiritual descendants of the early twentieth century progressives in the Chicago
Civic Federation and Citizens' Association of Chicago.[1] They were
strongly influenced towards constitutional revision by the writings
of constitutional scholar Kenneth Sears, who firmly believed that
in regard to its rigid constitution "Illinois, everything considered, is

---

[1] Some of the committee members were to play important roles in the politics
of Illinois and the nation. Stevenson became governor and two-time presidential
candidate, Kerner became governor, Witwer a candidate for the U.S. Senate and
president of the sixth constitutional convention held in Illinois, Mitchell national
chairman of the Democratic party, Cummings a solicitor general of the United
States, and Schaefer a justice of the Illinois Supreme Court.

in the worst position of any state of the Union."[2] Other pressures for constitutional revision came from the League of Women Voters, under the leadership of Mrs. Katherine Fisher and Mrs. Marian Farley, from Richard G. Browne, a professor at Illinois State University, and from journalists such as Irving Dilliard of the *St. Louis Post-Dispatch* and Carl Wiegman of the *Chicago Tribune*. Another advocate of constitutional change in the late 1940s was State Senator Richard J. Daley of Chicago.[3]

One of the committee's early decisions was to create a climate of concern about the need for constitutional change by constructing a literature of reform. At the urging of Sears, several committee members researched specific areas of constitutional problems, prepared papers, had them published in law reviews and journals and then reprinted for distribution to civic leaders and key politicians. Another task was to tackle the legislature again. In May 1947 Witwer journeyed to Springfield with several other committee members and testified before the Senate Executive Committee in favor of a convention call. Despite these efforts, no action was taken at that session.[4]

In 1949 the Committee on Constitutional Revision gained a powerful ally when Adlai E. Stevenson was sworn in as governor. The legislative program that Stevenson submitted to the General Assembly placed top priority on the calling of a constitutional convention. Stevenson's constitutional convention package was introduced in the House on February 4, 1949, and it included a bill revising the election laws to allow the proposition to be placed on the ballot under the party circle. A straight party vote would necessarily include a vote for or against the proposition depending upon the position adopted by each party at its state convention. A similar ballot arrangement had been largely responsible for the success of constitutional revision until passage of the Ballot Law of 1891. Stevenson received active support from the Illinois League of Women Voters and the Chicago Bar Association in his quest for a thorough review of what he termed an "almost insurmountable roadblock to

[2] Kenneth C. Sears and Charles V. Laughlin, "A Study in Constitutional Rigidity," *University of Chicago Law Review* 11 (1943):439.
[3] Samuel W. Witwer, personal interview, June 23, 1971.
[4] Van Allen Bradley, "State's Horse-and-Buggy Constitution Finally Revised by Bipartisan Effort," *Chicago Daily News*, November 14, 1954.

good government." One of Stevenson's early biographers characterized the opposition in this way:

> Much more strongly organized was the opposition, consisting of
> powerful labor, farm, and manufacturing pressure groups, plus a
> bloc of downstate lawmakers who feared that convention delegates
> would approve legislative reapportionment on an actual population
> basis, giving Cook County control of the legislature. There were
> fears by businessmen that a new constitution might pave the way
> for a state income tax, ... fears by some labor leaders that a new
> charter might wipe out labor's recent legislative gains, fears genuine
> or synthetic but loudly proclaimed that the bill of rights might be
> jeopardized, and protests that the proposed convention would cost
> from five to ten million dollars and would probably fail to produce
> an acceptable charter.[5]

Despite well organized support in the legislature and an attempt
at compromise by the deletion of the party circle provision, Stevenson's proposal was defeated on two votes in the House.[6]

GATEWAY AMENDMENT

Enthusiasm for the Stevenson proposal was diminished by the pres-
ence of a Republican alternative. Senate Republicans had introduced a resolution for a Gateway amendment as a substitute for the
convention call. They proposed to ease the requirement that constitutional amendments be approved by a majority of those voting
in the general election by allowing approval by two-thirds of those
voting on the amendment itself, thus eliminating the negative impact
of those failing to vote on the amendment question. Under this proposal an amendment could be approved by either counting method.
Further, the legislature could submit to the voters amendments to
three articles at a time, rather than just one. The proposal did not
alter the requirement for calling a constitutional convention, which
would still have to receive the favorable votes of a majority of all
persons voting in a general election. Nor did it change the restriction prohibiting amendments to the same article more than once
every four years.

[5] Kenneth S. Davis, *A Prophet in His Own Country* (Garden City, N.Y.:
Doubleday and Co., 1957), p. 343.
[6] Ibid., pp. 344–45.

Stevenson would have much preferred a constitutional convention, but after the defeat of his proposal, he announced his support for the Gateway amendment:

> We cannot wait forever for the most urgent constitutional reforms. . . . I doubt the sincerity of the 'Gateway proposal'. . . . It looks like an effort to dodge responsibility for blocking much-needed changes. . . . But in spite of my misgivings, I feel it is better to have something than nothing. . . . I will urge the Democratic party in an all-out nonpartisan effort to secure ratification of the Gateway Amendment by the voters in 1950.[7]

With Stevenson's support the Gateway amendment resolution easily passed both houses, receiving only two negative votes. The proposition would be submitted to the people in the November 1950 general election. In the meantime the General Assembly revised the election laws to provide for submission of constitutional propositions to the voters on a separate blue colored ballot. The use of the blue ballot was intended to increase voter awareness of the constitutional proposition and stimulate voter participation. At the polling place every voter would be handed a blue ballot, informed of its purpose, and instructed to return it to the election judge whether it was marked or not. The outside of the ballot bore the notice: "The failure to vote this ballot is the equivalent of a negative vote. . . ." In 1950 at least five other states used separate, colored ballots for constitutional propositions. The idea of a notice was borrowed from a similar practice used in Minnesota whose constitution also required approval of constitutional propositions by a majority of those voting in the election.[8]

The campaign for the Gateway amendment began shortly after the General Assembly had approved the amendment. The campaign was coordinated by the Illinois Committee for Constitutional Revision (ICCR), a group of statewide professional and civic organizations interested in the passage of Gateway. Samuel Witwer, who had been very active in the cause of constitutional reform as a chairman of the Committee on Constitutional Revision, was elected chairman. The ICCR conducted a well organized campaign which received

[7] Ibid., p. 346.
[8] Illinois Legislative Council, "Amending the Illinois Constitution," Memorandum 1–151, Springfield, March 1950.

the backing of both major political organizations, continuous editorial support and news coverage in major newspapers throughout the state, and the endorsement of all major labor, business, agricultural, professional, and civic organizations in Illinois. The committee supervised the distribution of an enormous quantity of campaign literature — posters, explanatory leaflets, and sample ballots, set up speaker's bureaus, and established local campaign committees in eighty-four of the state's 102 counties. The Gateway amendment was not tied to substantive issues, and support for its approval came from diverse sources whose specific interests may not have been coincident but who were all concerned with improving the prospects for constitutional change. After the Chicago Bar Association began to agitate for reform shortly after the close of World War II, interest in constitutional change grew. With a large boost from Adlai Stevenson, proponents of reform were in a position to reap the benefits of a generally recognized need to open up the amendatory process. In the November 1950 general election the voters overwhelmingly approved the Gateway amendment. Slightly more than 67 percent of those voting in the election cast affirmative votes for the proposition, and only 13 percent failed to vote.[9]

Popular approval of the Gateway amendment generated widespread hope that revision by amendment would once again become a feasible method for initiating constitutional change. Since the form of the ballot was changed in 1891, revision by amendment had not been an easy task. Of the fourteen amendments proposed between 1891 and 1950, only two had been adopted. Gateway amendments failed five times; proposed changes in the revenue article failed four times. The 1950 Gateway amendment became the first amendment proposal adopted in Illinois since 1908. Under its provisions, nine of the fourteen amendments submitted to the electorate between 1891 and 1950 would have been adopted.

The passage of Gateway was met with some reservation by those who felt that the new two-thirds requirement would still make it excessively difficult to obtain piecemeal constitutional change. On the

---

[9] Use of the blue ballot was undoubtedly a major cause for the high rate of voter participation on the amendment question. Between 1930 and 1946 when amendment proposals were printed on the regular ballot, non-voting averaged nearly 60 percent.

whole, however, Gateway was greeted with enthusiasm by proponents of constitutional revision. Obtaining the required popular vote appeared possible, although difficult. It also appeared that some of the delay in the amending process might be alleviated by the provision allowing amendments to three articles at any one time. Although the calling of a constitutional convention had been the primary goal of the civic and professional groups active in the years prior to 1950, the approval of Gateway seemed at the time to be a reasonable alternative.

REAPPORTIONMENT AMENDMENT

In his opening day address to the General Assembly on January 3, 1951, Governor Adlai Stevenson specifically delegated responsibility for selecting the first amendments to be submitted under Gateway to the members of the Sixty-seventh General Assembly.[10] Perhaps spurred on by the optimism generated by the passage of Gateway, the legislature subsequently passed four amendments to three articles of the constitution — the maximum allowed under the new provision. The four proposals would have (1) provided a new revenue article permitting the classification of property but prohibiting a graduated income tax, (2) amended the counties article to allow county sheriffs and treasurers to succeed themselves, (3) amended the counties article to remove the salary limitations on county officers, and (4) amended the corporations article to remove the double liability provision for state bank stock owners. At the following general election in November 1952, the first two proposals were defeated, failing to obtain approval by either two-thirds of those voting on the proposals or a majority of those voting in the election. The second two proposals gained approval under the new two-thirds provision of the Gateway amendment. Thus, Illinois's first experience with its liberalized amendatory process was at least a partial success, no doubt gratifying to advocates of constitutional reform.

The troublesome question of legislative reapportionment, the plague of state government for decades, was tackled in the next session of the legislature. By 1953, forty-two years had passed since the last reapportionment. According to the 1950 census, over half

[10] Illinois, Senate, *Journal,* 1951, pp. 1–37.

the state's population was located in Cook County, but under the
1901 apportionment it still had only nineteen of the fifty-one legislative districts. The great disparities within Cook County, and elsewhere in the state, in the population of districts also remained. Between the failure of the 1922 constitution and 1952, some twenty
resolutions proposing amendments to the legislative apportionment
article were introduced in the General Assembly but failed to pass.[11]

The passage of Gateway seemed to remove a major obstacle to a
new legislative apportionment in its liberalization of the amending
process. Several proposed reapportionment amendments were introduced in the 1951 legislative session but none was successful. In the
1953 session a reapportionment amendment backed by Republican
governor William Stratton was introduced into the legislature. It
passed the Senate easily. After an initial failure in the House, the
resolution was approved, 120 to 17.[12] Although the governor's support was the prime factor in passage, there was a feeling among
many legislators that popular approval might not be forthcoming,
and some may have voted for the measure expecting it to be defeated in the general election. On the whole, passage of the amendment was unexpected, since it would markedly change the status quo.

> Members were warned of the potential danger to their seats by the
> House minority leader, who characterized the amendment, on the
> floor of the House, as "the same thing as an employee signing his
> resignation." There was substantial opposition to the proposal in
> the General Assembly, and it could not have been passed without
> extensive logrolling, especially after a House Democratic conference
> was held wherein it was explained that it was not a party measure.[13]

Under the proposed amendment House districts were to be based
on population. New districts were established in 1955 and these
would be reapportioned in 1963 and every ten years thereafter. In
the Senate, districts were based on area, with Cook County and
Chicago allotted a certain specified number of districts. No provision
was made for altering Senate districts after 1955.

[11] Illinois Legislative Council, *Reapportionment in Illinois,* p. 12.
[12] Russell E. Olson, "Illinois Faces Redistricting," *National Municipal Review*
43 (July 1954):343–46.
[13] Gilbert Y. Steiner and Samuel K. Gove, *Legislative Politics in Illinois*
(Urbana: University of Illinois Press, 1960), p. 89.

Popular approval of the reapportionment amendment followed much the same pattern as that of the Gateway amendment. The ICCR was reactivated under the co-chairmanship of Witwer and Charles B. Shuman, president of the Illinois Agricultural Association. They would direct the ICCR in a vigorous campaign supported by major business, professional, and civic organizations in the state, and endorsed by both political parties. The backing ICCR received from these organizations helped dampen some of the opposition among members of the legislature. The reapportionment amendment also received substantial editorial support from Illinois newspapers. Chicago's four dailies and downstate dailies favored the amendment, though many weekly small town newspapers strongly opposed it.[14]

On November 2, 1954, after a well organized and highly publicized campaign, the voters of Illinois gave the reapportionment amendment a tremendous vote of approval. Of the 3,455,173 people voting in the election, 2,610,726 voted on the proposition, and 2,085,224 voted in the affirmative. The amendment passed under both counting methods, receiving 60 percent of the total vote cast and 80 percent of the vote cast on the proposal. In the downstate counties 64 percent of those voting on the proposal approved it, and in Cook County the comparable vote was an amazing 92 percent.[15] Two other amendments on the blue ballot, extending the term of the state treasurer from two to four years, and permitting the state to sell land in connection with the Illinois-Michigan Canal, also passed, receiving slightly smaller votes than the reapportionment amendment.

Passage of the reapportionment amendment did not assure successful reapportionment of the state. Only the action taken by the General Assembly could do that. The possibility that the legislature might fail to carry out the redrawing of House and Senate lines in 1955, or to redistrict the House afterwards, had been recognized by those who drew up the 1954 amendment. The amendment provided that if the legislature did not accomplish the prescribed redistricting, the governor should appoint a commission of ten mem-

[14] John E. Juergensmeyer, "The Campaign for the Illinois Reapportionment Amendment," mimeographed (Urbana: Institute of Government and Public Affairs, University of Illinois, 1957), pp. 29, 41.

[15] Ibid., pp. 34–36, 42.

bers, divided equally between the two major parties, and give them four months in which to produce a redistricting plan. If the commission failed, then all members of the chamber in question should be elected at large in the state. It was felt that the legislature, if threatened by reapportionment by a commission, would itself redistrict the state. Although the device worked in 1955 when the General Assembly succeeded in redrawing House and Senate districts, it did not work in 1963. Governor Kerner vetoed the legislature's measure, and the bipartisan commission failed to agree on a reapportionment plan. All 177 representatives were forced to run at large in the 1964 election.[16]

By 1965, when the at-large representatives elected under this system took their seats, reapportionment was no longer exclusively in the hands of the legislature or even the states. Decisions of the United States and Illinois supreme courts had overturned the provision of the 1954 amendment that Senate districts could be drawn on the basis of area. Following the one man, one vote principle for state legislative representation established in *Baker* v. *Carr* in 1962,[17] the United States Supreme Court in *Germano* v. *Kerner*[18] and the Supreme Court of Illinois in *People* ex rel. *Engle* v. *Kerner*[19] ruled that Senate as well as House districts should be based on population. After the 1965 General Assembly failed to devise a plan for Senate reapportionment, this was done by court action. The 1965 House reapportionment, worked out through a commission as the 1954 amendment had directed, was greatly dependent on the court's plan for Senate districts.[20]

The 1954 reapportionment plan, passed after such great efforts, failed to work. The chief difficulties arose because of party struggles for advantage and from the understandable desire of incumbent legislators to maintain the boundaries of the districts which had secured their election. Clearly, constitutional reform alone could not be expected to transform state government.

[16] David Kenney, "Representation in the General Assembly," in *Con-Con: Issues for the Illinois Constitutional Convention,* pp. 136–38.
[17] 369 U.S. 186 (1962).
[18] 378 U.S. 560 (1964), rehearing denied, 379 U.S. 875 (1965).
[19] 33 Ill. 2d 11, 210 N.E. 2d 165 (1965).
[20] Kenney, p. 139.

Judicial Amendment

Despite several setbacks, proponents of constitutional change felt genuinely optimistic about their experience with the amendatory process in the four years following the passage of Gateway. After the successful passage of the reapportionment and other amendments in 1954, they focused their efforts on attempts to amend the judicial and revenue articles of the 1870 constitution. Under the judicial article, judges at all levels in Illinois held office for limited terms and were nominated for office and elected on partisan tickets. Critics had long pointed out the need to separate judicial activity from political activity in the state.[21] There were other defects in the judicial article as well, but the major issue which divided judicial reformers was the choice between an appointed or an elected judiciary.[22] A proposed amendment drafted in 1953 by a joint committee of the Chicago and Illinois Bar Associations featured an appointed judiciary, and it was this feature that generated sufficient opposition in the legislature to defeat judicial reorganization in 1953. Opposition came generally from Chicago Democrats and downstate legislators. Governor William Stratton was officially neutral on the issue. The plan proposed by the committee and rejected by the legislature would have significantly altered the political status quo across the state. It was clear that the political leaders were not convinced by the committee recommendations or other reform pressures of the advisability of such a change. It was not until 1957, when the legislature finally approved a judicial amendment, that these political forces converged. Then, Governor Stratton and Richard J. Daley, Democratic mayor of Chicago, threw their weight behind the judicial amendment and it passed, although in substantially different form from the 1953 bar associations' committee proposal.[23] The 1957 amendment

[21] See, for example, Samuel Witwer, "The Illinois Constitution and the Courts," *University of Chicago Law Review* 15 (1947):57.

[22] This description of attempts at judicial reform through 1958 draws heavily from Steiner and Gove, pp. 164–98.

[23] The fact that the 1957 legislature was newly apportioned may have been an additional factor in achieving approval of the amendment. Alleviation of the great disparity between Cook County and downstate representation may have helped narrow the traditional cleavage between the two areas in the General Assembly, contributing to a more congenial legislative attitude toward judicial reorganization. However, as Steiner and Gove have pointed out, the two basic conditions necessary for approval were the support of the governor and support of the mayor of Chicago. Ibid., pp. 187–88.

left the question of selection and tenure up to the legislature with approval by the voters in a statewide referendum.

The organized campaign on behalf of the judicial amendment was based largely on previous experience with the Gateway and reapportionment campaigns. Heading up the statewide effort was a group called the Committee for Modern Courts. Heavy emphasis was placed upon the encouragement of local blue ballot committees which solicited the endorsement of local groups, formed speaker's bureaus, and distributed literature locally. The theme of the campaign was "Vote Yes on the Blue Ballot." There was little organized opposition in the state. Both political parties supported the amendment and the committee had received endorsements from ninety statewide organizations. However, there was scattered opposition among downstate politicians and a few lawyers and judicial officials.

In November 1958 the first comprehensive proposal for judicial change to be submitted to the voters since 1870 was closely defeated. By either counting method the amendment failed. It was approved by only 46 percent of those voting in the election and only 64 percent of those voting on the amendment question.[24]

Under the 1870 constitution, amendments could not be offered to the same article more often than once every four years. Thus, attempts at judicial reorganization would not be possible again until at least 1961. Pressures for reform did not abate after 1958, and in 1961 the General Assembly passed an amendment to the judicial article that closely paralleled the unsuccessful 1958 amendment. The amendment submitted to the voters in 1962 was intended to simplify the judicial system by centralizing its administration and eliminating overlapping jurisdictions. The new court system would be administered by the Illinois Supreme Court which would appoint an administrative director for daily administrative responsibilities. A single trial court, the circuit court, would replace the numerous police

[24] The closeness of the vote prompted several backers of the amendment to file suit claiming that the proposal had actually received a popular majority. The suit was taken to the Illinois Supreme Court to obtain a ruling that votes cast by voters who marked their ballots with a "√" rather than an "X" or simply wrote the word "yes" should have been counted. They believed that had these votes been counted the amendment would have passed. The claim was rejected by the court on January 20, 1960. *Schribner* v. *Sachs,* 18 Ill. 2d 400 (1960).

magistrate courts, justice of the peace courts, and county, probate, and criminal courts. The circuit court would consist of circuit court judges, associate circuit court judges, and magistrates appointed by the circuit court judges. Judges would be nominated and elected to begin with, but once elected each judge would run for reelection on his record. Names of judges would not appear on the retention ballot under a party label. The seven justices of the state supreme court would continue to be elected by district, but the districts were redistributed so that Cook County would have three instead of one and downstate would have four instead of six. There would also be a full-time appellate court. Previously county judges had served as appeal judges. Proponents of the amendment felt that the new system would reduce the costs and delays of litigation and insure greater political independence of the judiciary.

The statewide campaign for the amendment was once again coordinated by the Committee for Modern Courts, this time under the leadership of James Rutherford, a Chicago insurance executive. The committee followed much the same strategy as in 1958. The bipartisan campaign was formally launched in Springfield on May 19, 1962, at a meeting in the governor's mansion attended by leaders of both parties and representatives of the Illinois Bar Association. Speeches were given by Governor Otto Kerner, a Democrat, and Republican Secretary of State Charles F. Carpentier. Mayor Daley sent a message pledging his support.[25] By election time, seventy-six organizations representing agricultural, business, civic, religious, and labor interests pledged their support for the amendment. Both political parties also endorsed the amendment. Formal opposition came from eleven organizations, principally the Cook County Justices, Magistrates and Constables Association, and the County Officials Association of Illinois,[26] but opponents were not numerous and they never mounted an organized campaign effort.

The amendment passed by a comfortable margin in the November 1962 general election, approved by a majority of those voting in the election (57 percent), but falling just short (65 percent) of approval by two-thirds of those voting on the amendment.

[25] *St. Louis Post-Dispatch,* March 21, 1962.
[26] *Chicago Sun-Times,* November 3, 1962.

REVENUE AMENDMENT

Revenue had continued to be a source of controversy in Illinois. The major problems by the 1960s appeared to be the limitations on indebtedness and stipulations for uniform taxation of property, which led to numerous evasions; the dependence of the state for its revenues upon inequitable and regressive sales and property taxes; and the inadequacy of these taxes, which led to financial crises in every legislative session.

The state taxation issue concerned not only constitutional limitations, but uncertainty as to what those limitations were, as interpreted by the courts.[27] Attempts were made to remove these uncertainties by amending the revenue article. The proposed revenue article was the product of a series of developments that began in 1961 when Governor Otto Kerner took office. The state was facing a severe financial crisis. Expenditures had exceeded revenues ever since World War II, but the deficit had always been made up by a surplus in the General Revenue Fund which had been built up during the war when capital construction was at a standstill. By the time Kerner took office, that surplus had run out and the state faced a real shortage of funds. In the last few days of the 1961 session, the General Assembly finally enacted a series of administration proposals to increase existing rates on various taxes. The governor had proposed no basic changes in the tax structure, and the increases approved by the legislature only served to postpone a necessary decision on the adequacy of existing revenue sources.

By the close of the 1963 session of the legislature, interest groups, realizing that pressures for revenue reform were building, wanted to make sure they could accommodate that change.[28] This involved two loose coalitions of groups which over the years had been affected by Illinois tax policy. On the one hand, business groups tended to favor the existing system because they paid few direct taxes and these could be passed on to their customers. On the other hand, agriculture, labor, and education interests supported a redistribution of the

[27] Glenn W. Fisher, "Public Finance," in *Con-Con: Issues for the Illinois Constitutional Convention*, p. 294.

[28] Ann H. Elder and Glenn W. Fisher, *An Attempt to Amend the Illinois Constitution: A Study in Politics and Taxation* (Urbana: Institute of Government and Public Affairs, University of Illinois, 1969), pp. 12–24.

tax burden, agreeing on an income tax as the best way to achieve their various goals. The business coalition was the dominant force in state tax policy, and any realignment of the tax structure would have to be accomplished with their support. From March 1964 to February 1965 representatives from agriculture, education, labor, and business met regularly as the Selected Organizations Concerned with Amendment of the Revenue Article of the Illinois State Constitution to write a revenue article acceptable to all. Thus, before the next legislative session began, the major interest groups had made necessary compromises and struck crucial bargains. The groups involved took care to produce an amendment which would reflect as nearly as possible the interests of all organized groups likely to be affected.[29]

As the General Assembly turned its attention to the revenue question, it was clear that more dialogue was needed before an amendment would be approved. Differences centered around the issues of real estate classification and a state income tax. A joint legislative committee, with recommendations from the governor, agreed upon a flat-rate tax on individuals and corporations with a 6 percent ceiling; up to 3 percent could be levied by the legislature without a statewide referendum. In regard to real estate classification, the compromise which was finally adopted provided for classification in Cook County only. The proposal passed the House 143 to 18, with opposition coming from liberal Democrats who favored a graduated income tax and more flexibility in allowing the legislature to levy taxes, and from conservative Republicans who opposed any income tax. It passed the Senate 46 to 7 with all negative votes coming from Republicans.[30]

By the end of May 1966 Governor Kerner had appointed a committee of 100 civic leaders to lend a "citizen's flavor" to the campaign on behalf of the amendment. Another citizens' committee, which was formally incorporated and was made up of representatives of interest groups, actually had responsibility for running the campaign. This arrangement sometimes caused confusion since William J. Crowley, a vice-president of the Northern Illinois Gas Company, was chairman of both groups. Bozell and Jacobs, the

[29] Ibid., pp. 24–44.
[30] Ibid., pp. 51–64.

same public relations firm which had worked in the Gateway and reapportionment campaigns, was engaged. By this time local organizations in support of the measure were being developed throughout the state. Organization in rural areas was supervised by the Illinois Agricultural Association and in urban areas by the Illinois State Chamber of Commerce.[31]

As the history of constitutional revision in Illinois has aptly illustrated, change in the state's basic charter can come only in the absence of sustained opposition. It is the opposition much more than the support which is the critical factor in any referendum campaign. As it turned out, the negotiating process engaged in before and during the 1965 legislative session had not produced a compromise which was satisfying to all of the groups ultimately involved in creating state tax policy. One difficulty was the lack of publicity given the efforts of the Selected Organizations group before the session and subsequent drafting efforts during the session. Furthermore, the few lobbyists and legislators who actually drew up the amendment were not sufficiently representative of all salient interests. As a result, the public had only a vague idea of what was happening — a confusion compounded by the technical nature of the issue — and many groups vitally interested in tax policy were not represented. The compromise amendment agreed upon really satisfied none of the groups which would be affected by it. In the words of one observer, "too many gave up too much to get an amendment which was satisfactory to too few."[32]

The revenue amendment's chances for popular approval began to diminish as various groups and individuals announced their opposition. First, a small group of Democratic legislators denounced the amendment as restrictive and regressive and a step backward. The United Steelworkers announced their opposition on February 1, 1966, and were followed a month later by the executive board of the state AFL-CIO. At their convention in April the Illinois Congress of Parents and Teachers declared their opposition. The Independent Voters of Illinois also added their voice to the growing chorus of opponents, along with the League of Women Voters. The Illinois and Chicago Bar Associations were sharply split on the issue

[31] Ibid., pp. 69–72.
[32] Ibid., p. 102.

and neither was a significant factor in the campaign. Opposition had grown to the point where a formal organization, the Defeat the Revenue Article organization, was incorporated on September 20, 1966. Its existence and support by a wide variety of respected groups were an accurate index of the rough going faced by proponents of the amendment.

After an erratic campaign, in which both sides were hindered by lack of funds, the revenue amendment was defeated at the polls on November 8. It was approved by less than two-thirds (53 percent) of those voting on the amendment and less than a simple majority (42 percent) of those voting in the election. The rate of non-voting on the amendment was 22 percent.[33]

Post-Gateway Period — An Assessment

The Gateway amendment of 1950 obviously did not fulfill the hopes which had originally accompanied its passage. From 1950 to 1966, fifteen constitutional amendments were submitted to the voters; of these, six were approved and became part of the constitution. The provisions of Gateway were directly responsible for the success of only two of these six. Furthermore, of the successful amendments only two — reapportionment of the legislature in 1954 and the judicial article of 1962 — were of major significance. In the years since Gateway there was undoubtedly a revived interest in the amendatory process. Not only did the relative number of amendments submitted to the voters increase, but the proportion of amendments adopted was also slightly higher than in the years before Gateway. However, the fact remains that most of what has been accomplished was done during the years directly after passage of the amendment. Seven of the fifteen amendments submitted since Gateway were submitted by 1954, and all but two of these were approved. Of the eight amendments submitted in the intervening fifteen years only one has been successful. After the initial flush of

[33] Ibid., p. 91, and Thomas Kitsos, "Constitutional Amendments and the Voter, 1952–1966," Commission Papers of the Institute of Government and Public Affairs, University of Illinois (Urbana, 1968), p. 14. A second proposal on the ballot which would have amended the counties article to allow county sheriffs and treasurers to succeed themselves was also defeated. It was the third time since 1952 that this proposal had failed at the polls. Kitsos, p. 16.

success, the extensive revision that was to be the aftermath of Gateway did not materialize.

In a perceptive analysis of electoral behavior in all constitutional amendments submitted between 1952 and 1966, Thomas Kitsos identified certain patterns of voting behavior established by Illinois voters, and pointed out the inherent drawbacks to constitutional revision by the amendment process in Illinois.[34] His data indicated a clear division between downstate and Cook County voters. Normally, constitutional amendments received strong support from Cook County and strong opposition from the remaining downstate counties. He concluded that "Cook County 'yes' votes are counteracted by downstate 'no' votes to a certain extent and that the success or failure of an amendment proposal depends on the relative magnitude of those two opposing vote patterns. . . ."[35] There was no convincing evidence that proposals received any special advantage from being submitted in a presidential rather than a nonpresidential election year, or that single-proposal rather than multiple-proposal submission had any significant impact on the outcome of the election. Illinois voters were quite selective: Kitsos found that a relatively noncontroversial proposal might be aided if it accompanied an amendment that received a large favorable majority, but it was quite unlikely that a relatively unpopular proposal could slip by on the strength of a more popular proposal on the ballot. Voters were not particularly inclined to approve a proposition submitted for a second or third time. More often than not, propositions received higher votes the first time around. In evaluating the amendatory process after Gateway, Kitsos concluded that "under present amendment requirements, the 'piecemeal' approach to constitutional revision is a long and arduous process. . . . If [the pace since 1952] continues, significant revision of the constitution through the normal amending process will take an incredibly long time."[36] Kitsos's analysis added scholarly weight to the arguments of those who again directed their efforts towards a thorough revision of Illinois's constitution through the convention process.

[34] Ibid.
[35] Ibid., p. 7.
[36] Ibid., p. 20.

VII

The Sixth Constitutional Convention

TRENDS IN CONSTITUTIONAL REVISION

In the 1960s sentiment for constitutional change continued in Illinois as a result of two decades of effort by civic groups to provide a climate of opinion favorable to constitutional reform. This climate was also influenced by the renewed nationwide interest in state constitutional revision. During the middle and late 1920s, the thirties, and the early forties, no state had adopted a new constitution, although constitutions in Virginia (1928) and New York (1938) underwent extensive change. In the three following decades, however, constitutional reform burgeoned. Nineteen constitutional conventions were held from 1950 to 1968. Twenty-five hundred amendments to state constitutions were adopted in the same time period.[1]

Factors in this new constitutional reform movement included a growing interest in greater assumption of responsibility by the states, as well as the federal government, for what is now commonly referred to as the "urban crisis." In 1955, the Commission on Intergovernmental Relations (Kestnbaum Commission) called attention to the ways in which state constitutions restricted the scope, effectiveness, and adaptability of states and localities to respond to their problems. It suggested that "most states would benefit from a fundamental review and revision of their constitutions to make sure

[1] Albert L. Sturm, *Thirty Years of State Constitution-Making: 1938–1968* (New York: National Municipal League, 1970), p. v, 29–31, 55.

that they provide for vigorous and responsible government. . . ."[2] The National Municipal League increasingly directed its attention and research towards state constitutional problems, as did the Council of State Governments and the Chamber of Commerce of the United States. In 1967 the Committee for Economic Development issued a highly critical report on state governments and gave constitutional revision top priority among the corrective steps needed. The committee recommended that "most states should hold constitutional conventions, at the earliest possible date, in order to draft completely new documents." It warned that without thoroughgoing "revision of archaic constitutions and sweeping modernization of governmental institutions," the states would become little more than "administrative instrumentalities of decision-makers at other levels."[3] Another factor in increased revision efforts was the adoption of moderately forward-looking constitutions by the new states of Alaska and Hawaii. An important impetus was the Supreme Court. Its decisions in *Baker* v. *Carr* and other one man, one vote cases forced states to redistrict for more equal apportionment of state legislatures, increasing the responsiveness of legislators to demands for constitutional reform.

In this climate, the Illinois League of Women Voters, various members of the Chicago Bar Association, government officials, students of government, and scattered civic groups began an intensified campaign for constitutional reform in the 1960s. This campaign accelerated when Mrs. Marjorie Pebworth, former president of the League of Women Voters, was elected to the House of Representatives as a "blue ribbon" candidate in the 1964 at-large election. She recommended the formation of the Constitution Study Commission to the General Assembly and in 1965 became its first chairman. The commission consisted of twelve members of the legislature and six public members appointed by the governor. The General Assembly gave the commission a broad directive to examine all sections of the constitution, to determine where revisions should be made, and whether such changes would best be accomplished by

[2] Commission on Intergovernmental Relations, *A Report to the President for Transmittal to the Congress* (Washington, D.C., 1955), pp. 37, 56.
[3] Committee for Economic Development, *Modernizing State Government* (New York, 1967), pp. 22, 68.

amendment or by the calling of a convention. After two years of consideration, the commission concluded that "a constitutional convention is the best and most timely way to achieve a revised constitution." The commission recommended that the General Assembly place the question of calling a constitutional convention on the ballot in the November 1968 general election. It advised against placing any other amendments on the ballot, suggesting that "the electorate should not be asked to debate or rule on piecemeal amendments while a constitutional convention is being considered." The commission also recommended that its life be extended so that, should a convention be approved, the commission might provide delegates and members of the legislature with resource material on salient issues and problems of constitutional revision.[4]

Joint resolutions providing for a referendum on the question of calling a constitutional convention were introduced simultaneously in both houses of the General Assembly during the first week of the 1967 session. The convention call resolutions remained in committee until mid-April. The Senate resolution was recommended "do adopt" on April 12 and passed 50 to 0 six days later. The measure passed the House 150 to 14 on May 16. Thus, for the first time since 1934, the voters would have the opportunity to express their approval or disapproval of a convention call. The legislature also concurred with the Constitution Study Commission recommendation that no other amendments be submitted to the voters. The convention call would be the only blue ballot proposition in the November 1968 general election.

The success of the convention call in the General Assembly rested primarily on two factors. One was the desire of the members to honor the memory of Mrs. Pebworth, who died suddenly during her second term in the House of Representatives. Her dedicated and energetic efforts on behalf of the convention call were widely recognized, and passage of the convention resolution was in large part a tribute to her efforts. Secondly, many members were apparently willing to vote for the measure because they felt its chances for popular approval were slim.

[4] Illinois, Constitution Study Commission, *Report Submitted to the 75th General Assembly* (February 1967), p. 7.

CAMPAIGN FOR THE CONVENTION

In approving the convention call resolution, the legislature made no provision for insuring adoption of the proposition.[5] As in the past, the campaign was to be a civic matter, with only minimal direct government involvement. Shortly after the adjournment of the General Assembly, an informal group, spearheaded by Louis Ancel, Mrs. Peggy Norton, James T. Otis, Mrs. Mary Helen Robertson, Elroy C. Sandquist, Jr., Peter Tomei, Samuel W. Witwer, and several others who had been closely involved on both sides of past amendment campaigns, began meeting with representatives of organizations that could be expected to concern themselves with the convention call. This was the genesis of the Illinois Committee for Constitutional Convention (ICCC), which became the clearinghouse for and manager of the referendum campaign. The group was given quasi-official status when, at the request of its steering committee, Governor Otto Kerner appointed Kingman Douglass, Jr., a Chicago investment banker, and William J. Kuhfuss, president of the Illinois Agricultural Association, as campaign co-chairmen. The governor also announced the selection of a board of directors as well as the other committee officers. Samuel Witwer was to serve as general counsel, Emory Williams of Sears, Roebuck and Co. as treasurer, Mrs. Robertson of the League of Women Voters as secretary, and Mrs. Norton of the Illinois Parent Teachers Association as executive secretary. William W. Allen of the Illinois Agricultural Association was later appointed as campaign manager for the committee. On April 16, 1968, the campaign was formally initiated at a luncheon in the governor's mansion in Springfield. In attendance were members of the committee and other interested organizations, political leaders, and members of the press.

The ICCC operated what was perhaps the most vigorous and best planned campaign ever conducted for a constitutional proposal in Illinois. By adhering to some key strategy decisions, by employing both proven methods and at least one new campaign device, and by capitalizing on the meaning Illinois voters attached to the blue

[5] This account of the campaign for adoption of the convention call is taken from Joseph P. Pisciotte, "How Illinois Did It," *National Civic Review* 58 (July 1969):291–96, and a memo from Mrs. Peggy Norton, executive secretary of the Illinois Committee for Constitutional Convention, typewritten (n.d.).

ballot, the committee was able to offset a major constitutional restriction as well as a negative attitude toward such change among
large segments of the population. As Gateway's relaxed rules for
passage of constitutional issues did not apply to convention calls,
passage would be imperiled by the great numbers who would vote
in the election but would fail to vote on the convention call question.
The problem was further intensified by the fact that 1968 was a
presidential election year when, although voter turnout was at its
peak, most voters, the political parties, and the news media were
concerned primarily with the candidates for state and national
offices.

The $250,000 campaign was financed primarily by contributions
from individual citizens and private business. In addition to the
usual expenses for office operations, the money was used for publication and distribution of campaign materials, advertising in the news
media, organization and coordination of local campaigns, employment of field workers and a public relations firm, and survey research. The use of survey research by a convention call or amendment campaign committee was a first in Illinois. Three statewide
surveys would be conducted to provide information on which to
operate the campaign.

The first poll was designed by the Institute of Government and
Public Affairs of the University of Illinois and carried out by the
university's Survey Research Laboratory in the summer of 1968.
Its purpose was to determine two basic elements — the voters'
awareness of the convention call, and their attitude toward the call
at that point in the campaign process. The second and third studies
were carried out by a private research firm. One was conducted in
July and August 1968 to obtain in-depth information on voter
awareness and perception, and ballot strength of the convention call.
It was also designed to test potential campaign themes and slogans.
The last survey was conducted immediately after the election. Its
purpose was to pinpoint elements in the campaign which had aided
passage of the convention call and those which had been detrimental
or of little value.

Data from the surveys led directly to the formulation of two key
campaign decisions. One was to gear the campaign to increase voter
turnout and participation on the issue. Judging from data obtained

in the second survey, the strategists assumed that a relatively fixed number of no votes would be cast and that a higher rate of participation on the issue would result in a significant rise in the number of yes votes. Study of the November election results showed that the proposition attracted the attention of 87.5 percent of the voters; of these, 72 percent voted for and 28 percent voted against the convention.

The second successful strategy was the decision to keep the convention call issue completely nonpartisan and not allow it to become tied to any political party, candidate, group, or issue. The campaign was therefore based on the idea that a convention should be called to take a look at Illinois's 100-year-old constitution. The post-election survey data confirmed the soundness of this decision. Ninety-five percent of those who voted for the convention call did so because they saw the constitution as outdated, in need of revision, or too old.

The surveys also revealed that the separate blue ballot, required under Illinois election law for constitutional amendments and convention calls, had become symbolic of improvement and reform in Illinois government. Further, it showed that the blue ballot, regardless of past amendment campaigns, had not become identified with any substantive issue, and thus could be used extensively by the ICCC to perpetuate the good government image sought by its basic strategies.

These public relations techniques were undoubtedly a vital factor in the success of the convention call in the age of Madison Avenue campaigns. However, the public relations men were given a promising situation built up over the years by the persistence of constitutional reformers, and reinforced by constitutional change in other states. Gaining support from the news media was vitally important, but this task too had largely been accomplished through years of convincing editors and columnists of the need for constitutional revision. Advocates of constitutional change also contributed to the absence of organized support against the call by their careful cultivation of political leaders and their knowledge of the location of political power in the state. Both political parties, most incumbents and candidates for major office, and civic and professional organizations endorsed the convention call. Some opposition came from the state AFL-CIO, the Illinois State Association of Township Supervisors, and a group known as Save Our Suburbs (SOS), but none of these groups conducted an organized opposition campaign.

Of the 4.7 million people voting in the November 1968 election, 2.9 million voted yes on the convention call — slightly over 60 percent, and well over the necessary majority of those voting in the election. Only 590,000 voters failed to mark their blue ballots. The margin of victory, over 600,000 votes, constituted the greatest plurality ever given a constitutional proposal in Illinois.

DELEGATE SELECTION

Following the recommendation of the 1965 Constitution Study Commission, the Seventy-fifth General Assembly created a second commission to advise the legislature and the governor on an enabling act for the election of delegates and organization of the convention. Sixteen legislators and ten public members were appointed to the commission. Thomas G. Lyons, former Democratic state senator from Chicago who served as vice-chairman with Representative Pebworth on the first commission, was elected chairman. Among the public commission members were Louis Ancel, Mrs. Alice Ihrig, Mrs. Dawn Clark Netsch, James T. Otis, and Samuel Witwer, all of whom had long been involved in constitutional reform. The Institute of Government and Public Affairs of the University of Illinois was engaged as commission staff.[6]

Overshadowing the deliberations of the Lyons commission was the threat of convention failure. Although Hawaii and Pennsylvania had realized recent successes, the products of conventions in Rhode Island, New York, and Maryland had been defeated at the polls. The convention planners in Illinois attempted to learn from the mistakes of other states as well as from those made in the 1920–22 Illinois convention. For example, the enabling act sought to avoid

[6] For an account of the commission's membership, activities, and detailed recommendations, see Illinois, Constitution Study Commission, *Report: Preparing for the Illinois Constitutional Convention* (Chicago, 1969). A third commission, chaired by Senator Robert Coulson of Waukegan, was created by the 76th General Assembly to make arrangements for some of the more immediate needs of the convention. For an account of its activities and recommendations, see Illinois, Constitution Study Commission, *Report: Launching the Sixth Illinois Constitutional Convention; the Last Giant Step!* (Springfield, 1970).

a "rich man's convention" and the problem of absenteeism which had plagued the 1920–22 convention, by providing a respectable salary for delegates and some incentive for regular attendance. The enabling legislation of 1969 allowed the delegates a basic salary of $625 per month.[7] Although the legislation did not stipulate the length of the convention, the $625 salary would continue for only eight months. In addition, convention members were paid $75 for each day they attended plenary sessions or committee meetings, with a 100-day maximum. Delegates also received allowances for travel, room and board, and postage. State legislators and other public officials could receive only the postage, mileage, and expense allowance.

Judicial interpretations of the enabling act were crucial to the nature of delegate selection. Because of conflicting views on the provisions in the 1870 constitution, one of the major issues was whether public officials could serve as delegates. The Illinois Supreme Court in a friendly suit argued by James T. Otis[8] ruled that neither the governor, lieutenant governor, auditor of public accounts, secretary of state, superintendent of public instruction, nor attorney general could serve as delegates. The court also held that a judge would have to vacate his judicial office if he sat as a member of the convention, and that any person convicted of an infamous crime or any officer who had misused public funds or been impeached could not serve as a delegate. All other public officials, including state legislators, could be convention delegates without pay.

The enabling act called for a primary and a general election, both to be conducted on a nonpartisan basis. The nonpartisan provision was challenged in the same suit under the constitutional prescription that delegate elections must be "conducted in the same manner" as the partisan elections for state senators. The court rejected the argument, holding that "in the same manner" meant only that delegates must be elected by the people, in free and equal elections, by ballot. Thus Illinois was to have its first completely nonpartisan delegate election since 1818.

The provision of the enabling act which caused the greatest controversy was the placement of candidates' names on the election

[7] *Laws of Illinois,* 1969, pp. 57–67.
[8] *Livingston v. Ogilvie,* 43 Ill. 2d 9.

ballots. The act stipulated that in the primary election the name of the person first filing his nominating petition with the secretary of state would be certified first on the ballot. The names of the other candidates were to be listed in the order that their nominating petitions were filed with the secretary of state. However, as a result of a dispute involving mailed petitions and those delivered to the state capitol in person, the legislative procedure was altered by the United States Court of Appeals.[9] The court required the secretary of state to draw lots to determine the candidates' ballot position.

For the general election the enabling act required that in those districts where a primary was held,[10] the person who received the highest number of primary votes was to be certified first on the ballot. The other candidates would be listed according to the number of primary votes they received. In the eight districts where no primary election was held, the act required that the same procedure be followed as that originally provided by the legislature for the primary elections. The United States District Court, however, overturned this provision and required that in these districts, the order of ballot position was to be determined by lottery.

Over five hundred candidates filed petitions for the 116 delegate positions in fifty-eight districts. Illinois voters, however, did not match the intense interest shown by potential candidates in the delegate contests. Public meetings held by candidates often attracted such poor attendance that the audience was outnumbered by the candidates themselves.[11] Voting in the primary and general delegate elections was the lightest in recorded electoral history in the state of Illinois. Voter turnout averaged 18 percent in the September 23 primary election and 27 percent in the November 18 general election.[12]

The absence of party labels did not mean, of course, that parties were not involved in delegate campaigns. The Chicago Democratic organization slated candidates as it did for any partisan elec-

[9] *Leahy* v. *Powell,* No. 2259–69 (Sangamon County, filed July 10, 1969).

[10] Primaries were not held in the eight senatorial districts where four or fewer persons filed petitions as delegate candidates. Thomas R. Kitsos and Joseph P. Pisciotte, *A Guide to Illinois Constitutional Revision: The 1969 Constitutional Convention* (Urbana: Institute of Government and Public Affairs, University of Illinois, 1969), p. 26.

[11] See, for example, *Chicago Today,* August 31, 1969.

[12] Illinois, Secretary of State, *Official Vote* (1970).

tion, and the successful nominees included David Stahl, Mayor Daley's administrative officer, and Richard M. Daley, son of the mayor.[13] Downstate Republican and Democratic candidates made strong efforts to get the blessings of their party leaders. However, the nonpartisan character of the election did encourage the candidacy of independent civic leaders who were not closely connected with either party. The nonpartisan election also gave party members who were not ticketed by organization leaders a chance. Several Chicago Democrats who were not slated by the party ran anyway and defeated the organization candidates in their districts. These included delegates with particular interests and expertise in the constitutional field, such as Peter Tomei, chairman of the Constitutional Study Committee of the Chicago Bar Association; Mrs. Dawn Clark Netsch, member of the General Assembly's Constitution Study Commission; Albert Raby, Elmer Gertz, and Bernard Weisberg, each with longtime service in the field of civil rights and civil liberties; Ronald C. Smith, Professor of Law at John Marshall School of Law; and attorney Mrs. Mary Lee Leahy, member of the Independent Democratic Coalition with a particular interest in environmental protection. The same thing happened in many downstate districts. Voters in a traditionally Republican district, for example, usually chose Republican delegates, but not necessarily the party regulars whom the Republican organization would have preferred. In this way the nonpartisan method of electing delegates contributed greatly to the individuality and diversity of the convention delegation.

The delegates who gathered in Springfield for orientation meetings on December 5, 1969, were more varied in occupation, sex, and race than any previous constitutional convention delegation in Illinois. Although in their backgrounds the delegates were not typical of the state's population (96 of the 116 members were college graduates and income level was above average), they did represent groups in Illinois most interested in public service and constitutional reform. Fifty-six lawyers served as delegates, maintaining the dominance of the legal profession in Illinois constitution making. However, new

[13] Illinois, Secretary of State, *Members: Illinois Constitutional Convention, 1969–1970.*

groups also played a major part. Eleven educators took part as delegates, indicating the greater concern which the education profession
felt about government problems, and the increased prestige of educators as experts, fit to determine the constitutional future of Illinois
citizens. Only five farmers served as delegates, indicating a reverse
trend for agriculture. Another increasingly important occupational
field was the wide area of governmental employment. Eleven delegates worked either for city, county, or state government. Other
occupations further indicated the complexity of mid-twentieth century society. Three delegates were employed in the tax field, five
were bankers, and four were in advertising and public relations. One
delegate was an accountant, one an office manager, one a newspaper
editor, one a minister, and only two, James Kemp and William
Lennon, were labor union executives.[14]

Women were represented for the first time in Illinois constitution
making. The fifteen women delegates, like the men, came from
varied backgrounds and practiced diverse occupations. Several were
attorneys. Mrs. Dawn Clark Netsch was a law professor, Mrs. Gloria
Pughsley was employed by the City of Chicago in community activities, Mrs. Maxine Wymore was a juvenile probation officer, and
Mrs. Betty Howard owned and operated a public relations firm.
Several other women delegates had long records of volunteer work
in civic positions. Many had been associated with the League of
Women Voters in its efforts for constitutional revision. Two of the
women were also part of the thirteen-member black delegation. With
one exception all the blacks and the women delegates came from
Chicago or from other districts in the northern third of the state.

The 1970 delegation was considerably younger than that of the
1920–22 convention. Thirty-four of the delegates were under forty
years of age. The youngest delegate, James Gierach, was only
twenty-five years old, while the oldest, J. L. Buford, was seventy-
two. Most of the delegates were born in Illinois, but others claimed
birth places in as many as seventeen different states. One Chicago
delegate, Victor Arrigo, was born in Sicily; another, David Linn,
was born in Poland. Other delegates were second or third generation
descendants of European immigrants.

[14] Ibid.

Delegates who were also serving in Illinois legislature included Paul Elward and Victor Arrigo, both Democrats from Cook County. Several delegates were former legislators, including John Parkhurst of Peoria, David Davis of Bloomington, Elbert Smith of Decatur, John Leon and Thomas Lyons of Chicago, Robert Canfield of Rockford, and Dwight Friedrich of Centralia. Elbert Smith had served as auditor of public accounts for the state, and Edward Jenison of Paris was both a former United States congressman and state legislator.

Delegates Franklin Dove of Shelbyville and Henry Green of Urbana gave a certain historical continuity to the convention. Both were namesakes of grandfathers who had served in the 1920–22 convention.[15] Delegate Davis was the great grandson of David Davis, Justice of the U.S. Supreme Court, U.S. Senator, and member of the Illinois constitutional convention of 1847.

CONVENTION PROCEEDINGS

A historical touch was given to the opening of the convention by the enabling act's stipulation that the delegates would convene in the House of Representatives chambers in Springfield on December 8, 1969 — the one hundredth anniversary of the convening of delegates for the 1869–70 convention. All the pageantry was in evidence that first day: state officials attended the proceedings, Governor Ogilvie presided, a gavel belonging to the late Mrs. Pebworth was presented to the convention, and delegates' remarks indicated that they were duly impressed by their position and the task ahead. This mood was interrupted only by Richard M. Daley's unsuccessful motion to censure the governor for remarks made prior to the convention.[16]

The harmonious atmosphere quickly faded in the struggle to establish rules and organize the convention. In the past convention organization had been crucial both to the quality of the convention's work and to its public acceptance. During the three-day delegate

---

[15] The elder Mr. Dove, a member of the 1920–22 convention, attended the 1970 convention and spoke to the delegates as an honored guest. Sixth Illinois Constitutional Convention, *Record of Proceedings: Verbatim Transcripts,* March 20, 1970. Hereafter cited as *Verbatim Transcripts.*

[16] *Verbatim Transcripts,* December 8, 1969.

orientation session on December 5 through 7 most delegates were approached about various methods of organizing, and an outline began to take shape. Though some delegates challenged Samuel Witwer as candidate for convention president, his election was ultimately unanimous. Witwer's prestige among the delegates and the public by his long years of hard work in the field of constitutional revision, his knowledge of constitutional law, and his political activity as a candidate for the U.S. Senate, gave him an edge over other candidates. Witwer was also determined to see that the convention, if at all possible, produce a document acceptable to Illinois voters. These qualities in the president were to be important factors in the convention's results.

The delegates generally accepted the need for a bipartisan organization of the convention. Witwer was a Republican, so the obvious choice for vice-president was a Democrat, and the obvious Democrat was the leader of the Chicago Democratic delegation, Thomas Lyons. However, Lyons and Witwer were both from Cook County. To keep a balance in the convention, two additional vice-presidencies were created. Elbert Smith of Decatur, who had been making a strong bid for convention leadership, won one of the positions. This left the lower half of the state unrepresented, a situation resolved with the election of John Alexander, resident of the rural community of Virden, south of Springfield. The choice of the twenty-eight-year-old Alexander also fulfilled a demand that the needs of youth be acknowledged in the convention's deliberations. The convention recognized two other delegate groups with its election of Odas Nicholson, black woman attorney, to the newly created post of convention secretary.[17]

The convention tried to maintain the harmonious bipartisan spirit with which the opening day festivities and organization had begun.

[17] The enabling act had not specifically provided for additional officers. However, Attorney General Scott ruled that the convention did have the right to establish these officers and pay them. He declared that "when the People elect delegates to forge for them a new Constitution, they are exercising their power in a most unique and singular fashion. The authority the electorate grants the Constitutional Convention to restructure their form of government is the most fundamental power of government the People can bestow. And virtually the only effective limit on it is the right of the electorate to ratify or reject the end product of the Convention's efforts." (*Verbatim Transcripts*, December 16, 1969).

Marked attention was paid to keeping a favorable public attitude toward the convention and its work. In this effort, as in the campaign for a convention call, public relations techniques and educational facilities and talents were put to work. The delegates received materials from the second and third Constitution Study Commissions.[18] In addition, the governor's Constitution Research Group of scholars prepared eighteen background papers on major constitutional issues, which were bound for use by the delegates and issued to the general public.[19]

The full use of public relations facilities and techniques resulted in the most publicized convention in Illinois history.[20] The convention's public information committee, headed by David Stahl, established a public telephone information service, provided a documentary film for use in classrooms and by community organizations, and mailed weekly news summaries to newspapers and television and radio stations. Delegates and convention staff members kept close personal contact with news media representatives at the convention. To keep their constituents posted on convention happenings, delegates wrote columns in their local newspapers, made speeches, and appeared at meetings. Other groups which were vitally interested in the convention, including the League of Women Voters, the state federations of labor, the Chamber of Commerce, the Welfare Council of Metropolitan Chicago, and the Illinois Agricultural Association, also prepared periodic reports to inform their members and keep public interest alive.

The convention also conducted public hearings in cities throughout the state, attended by members of the convention's substantive committees and by a total of seven thousand citizens. Over one thousand witnesses testified at these regional hearings, and another

[18] Among these were George D. Braden and Rubin G. Cohn, *The Illinois Constitution: An Annotated and Comparative Analysis;* Janet Cornelius, *A History of Constitution Making in Illinois;* and Illinois, Constitution Study Commission, *Illinois Constitutional Revision: A Bibliography* (ed. Susan Welch), later revised and enlarged by Charlotte B. Stillwell and Stanley E. Adams as *The Constitution of Illinois: A Selective Bibliography.*

[19] These papers were published by the University of Illinois Press as *Con-Con: Issues for the Illinois Constitutional Convention,* ed. Samuel K. Gove and Victoria Ranney (Urbana, 1970).

[20] David E. Stahl, "Public Information," *Illinois Constitutional Convention Summary* no. 32 (September 3, 1970), p. 17.

eight hundred were heard by the substantive committees in Spring-field.[21] The goal of this activity was to give Illinois citizens direct access to convention proceedings, and to keep the convention before the public as an open deliberative body, truly considering the issues as they were presented, not acting on decisions already made in back room party caucuses.

This open, nonpartisan image was more than a public relations facade. Politics and political groups did have a major impact on convention deliberations, but the convention did not become polarized into tightly organized partisan groups. Although Republicans had a numerical majority at the convention, they seldom organized to take advantage of it, due to ideological and geographical schisms. The thirty-one to thirty-five regular Cook County Democrats generally voted as a bloc on major issues. However, since this group, even with frequent downstate Democratic support, could not swing the convention to its wishes, its influence had to be expressed cautiously. Eleven of the thirteen black delegates caucused together, but frequently voted with the other Chicago Democrats. Only on the bill of rights clause against discrimination on the basis of sex did women, spearheaded by Odas Nicholson and Betty Howard, make their influence felt as a group. The most cohesive group in regard to voting patterns was the nine independent Democrats who had run against organization candidates in Chicago. Because of their abilities and their unity, they functioned at times as a balance of power, holding more than their share of committee leadership positions and often exerting decisive influence in debates. Still, no individual or group could be depended upon to vote a certain way every time. Coalitions and alignments shifted with each issue. Critical observers, accustomed to legislative sessions where party leadership and caucuses directed a more orderly process, grimly anticipated that the convention would never accomplish its goals within any reasonable deadline and would be finally forced to behind-the-scenes concessions to major power blocs.

There were times when the dissatisfactions of the delegates and their lack of cohesiveness seemed about to fulfill the critics' predications and close down the proceedings, the same conditions which

[21] This information is taken from unpublished reports of the convention.

had resulted in lengthy adjournments in the 1920–22 convention. Dissatisfaction in January with Witwer's choice of committee appointments coalesced in March with discontent over his efforts to hurry deliberations. At this time the convention was forced to vacate the General Assembly chambers to make room for the legislature, and it was decided to move the convention into the Old State Capitol, originally built in 1839 and newly renovated as a historical monument.

Many delegates objected to the move to the Old State Capitol. Some felt the facilities were inadequate, others that removing the convention from the political atmosphere of the legislative halls took it away from the real conflicts in Illinois. Others, however, considered the move a major positive factor in the convention's results.[22] Earlier efforts in other states to remove conventions from legislative chambers had demonstrated distinct advantages. New Jersey's successful 1947 convention was located on the campus of Rutgers University "to get it and its members out of the atmosphere of the State House and its pervasive aroma of legislative maneuvering, midnight lobbying, and official protectiveness." Alaska's 1955–56 convention, at the University of Alaska, enabled the delegates "to develop a sense of community in the service of Alaska as a whole" which would have been difficult to achieve in the legislative environment of the state capitol.[23] The removal of the 1970 Illinois convention from the State House in Springfield, even though the move was only a few blocks, had these same advantages.

The new location had the added advantage of giving the delegates a sense of continuity with Illinois's past. They were constantly reminded that Abraham Lincoln had sat as a state legislator in the very chamber in which they convened, and that he had given his "house divided" speech there at the close of the Republican state convention in 1858. They were also reminded that theirs was the fourth constitutional convention to sit in those chambers, and were urged to make their work meaningful and productive in comparison to earlier efforts. From the time of the move to the Old State Capitol,

[22] Personal interviews with Samuel Witwer and Joseph Pisciotte, June 1971.

[23] John E. Bebout and Emil J. Sady, "Staging a State Constitutional Convention," in *Major Problems in State Constitutional Revision*, ed. W. Brooke Graves (Chicago: Public Administration Service, 1960), p. 76.

convention leaders saw a change in many delegates — a determination that the convention should not fail and should accomplish substantial and effective constitutional change.

Perhaps the convention's moment of truth and its closest point to dissolution came in the closing weeks, when the delegates worked through two politically loaded issues — the method of electing members of the House of Representatives and the method of judicial selection. Separate but related moves were made to replace cumulative voting with election of representatives from single-member districts and to supplant election of judges with an appointive system. Chicago Democrats fought to retain cumulative voting, and most Republicans and downstate Democrats advocated single-member districts. Chicago Democrats were also the strongest advocates of the existing judicial system, and resisted all attempts to change it. Legal reformers had long advocated removing the judiciary from the elective political system. Furthermore, the resignation of two state supreme court judges amidst charges of impropriety shortly before the convention began had aroused public sentiment for some sort of merit selection system for judges. However, nominations for judicial positions were a mainstay of political patronage, and Chicago Democrats were determined to maintain the elective judicial system. Democrats clashed with reform groups, most Republicans, and the independents, all of whom advocated merit selection.

Convention leaders felt that these two issues should be among those submitted separately to the voters. Illinois constitutional history, as well as the failure of the Maryland and New York single-package constitutions, had shown that separate submission of controversial issues improved the constitution's chances for acceptance. The original plan for each of the two issues was to include one alternative in the body of the constitution and submit the other alternative separately — for example, to include elective judges in the body of the constitution with a separate vote for merit selection which, if approved by the voters, would replace the elective provision. The conflict arose over which alternative should be included in the body of the document — which would increase its chances for approval. Only last-minute work by the convention leadership and a bipartisan coalition of delegates from throughout the state effected a compromise solution. The two alternatives for each of the disputed questions would be submitted separately to the voters. Voters would be asked to choose between Options 1-A (cumulative voting) and 1-B (single-member districts) for the election of representatives, and between Options 2-A (election) and 2-B (merit selection) for the selection of judges.[24] The coalition which brought about this compromise juggled votes, pleaded, threatened, and engaged in intricate parliamentary maneuvering to keep their compromise intact. The solution remained shaky until the end of an eighteen-hour marathon session when the final vote sent the ballot to the Style and Drafting Committee at 3:00 A.M. on September 1.[25]

CONSTITUTION OF 1970

The openness and lack of polarization in the convention had its beneficial aspects for the proposed 1970 constitution. Open sessions won approval of newspaper writers, which was crucial in establishing favorable public attitudes towards the proposed document. Also, the absence of tight organization and secret caucuses gave the delegates an opportunity to confront the issues. The benefits of this opportunity were apparent in many aspects of the convention's completed document.

The bill of rights provided the best example of the benefits of open discussion. The Committee on the Bill of Rights brought together strong-minded representatives of most Illinois groups which were concerned about the issues. Chairman Elmer Gertz, Bernard Weisberg, general counsel for the Illinois branch of the American Civil Liberties Union, and Albert Raby, black activist in the civil rights field, met on the same committee with Thomas Kelleghan, probably the most conservative member of the convention, and Father Francis X. Lawlor, who had led South Side Chicago neighborhood block clubs against integrated housing. Another notable committee member was Victor Arrigo, whose major goal at the convention was to protect the reputation of Italian Americans in Illinois. Arrigo also sided with Father Lawlor in leading a vigorous anti-abortion campaign during committee hearings. Also among the

---

[24] If neither option received a majority from those voting in the election, the 1870 provisions on each issue would have remained.

[25] *Verbatim Transcripts*, September 1, 1970.

committee members were Virginia Macdonald, the committee's only woman, James Kemp, a labor union official, and Arthur Lennon, a controversial but able attorney from Joliet.

Bill of Rights Committee hearings were often fractious and frequently dramatic, but their product was an article substantially changed from the 1870 bill of rights. Gertz, Weisberg, and others hailed the new bill of rights as one of the best in the nation, with tremendous potential for protection and extension of individual rights.[26] Among other changes, the new article added equal protection of the laws to the due process clause, expanded the provision against unreasonable searches and seizures to include "invasions of privacy or interceptions of communications by eavesdropping devices or other means," and wrote in an enlightened concept of the purpose of penalties after criminal conviction. One of the most far-reaching provisions in the bill of rights — and perhaps in the entire constitution — attempted to deal with continuing racial tensions. This major statement provided freedom from discrimination in hiring and promotion practices and in housing. A companion statement insured equal protection of the laws regardless of sex, an acknowledgment of the influence of women's liberation groups. Another forbade discrimination against the handicapped.

These provisions were examples of ways in which Illinois constitution makers in 1969–70 struggled to respond to pressures of the times in their attempt to create a relevant, publicly acceptable document. Despite a desire to incorporate only broad statements of policy in the new constitution, the convention necessarily became involved with current issues. Arrigo's clause condemning communications that undermine "individual dignity" was included in the bill of rights mainly because few delegates wanted to vote against such a concept, despite the difficulty of interpreting it in the courts. Similarly, the completed bill of rights assured that the individual's right to keep and bear arms could be infringed only by the state's police power. Gun control was such a pressing issue in many downstate areas that ignoring it might have been a fatal blow to the proposed constitution's chances.

[26] Elmer Gertz, "Bill of Rights," *Illinois Constitutional Convention Summary* no. 32 (September 3, 1970), p. 4; Bernard Weisberg, "Article I — Bill of Rights," *Chicago Bar Record,* 52 (November 1970):63–69.

The convention recognized another current public interest in its passage of an environment article declaring the state's and individual citizen's duty to ensure a healthful environment. This concept was not unique to Illinois, but a provision that individuals could enforce this right against other individuals or against a governmental unit through appropriate legal proceedings was not found in any other state constitution in 1970. A general provision asserting the importance of public transportation as an essential purpose for which public funds could be expended was a further recognition of contemporary national and state needs and interests.

Apart from the bill of rights and the environment article, though, the delegates were often frustrated in their efforts or even their desire to accomplish substantive constitutional change. This was a difficulty in twentieth century constitution making in other states as well as in Illinois. Constitutional reformers wanted state constitutions to be broad, flexible statements of organic law, but the public reverence for constitutions as repositories of traditional wisdom, together with opposition from groups which benefitted from out-dated provisions, often put the reformers' goal beyond reach. More difficult were the structural reforms which were being demanded by those dissatisfied with government's response to a changing world. The failure in 1968 of the Maryland reform constitution indicated that any attempt to streamline government and make it less expensive and possibly more responsive to the people would be almost impossible to achieve. As constructive and beneficial to the general public as many structural reforms might be, too many groups depended on the status quo and capitalized on the inertia of the average voter for any major changes in state and local government to be realized.

This difficulty was illustrated in the executive article, which largely avoided the short ballot issue. The delegates did alter the method of choosing executive officers so that the governor and lieutenant governor would be elected as a team. This change was clearly a reaction to the situation at the time the delegates were meeting, when a Republican governor and a Democratic lieutenant governor were in office. The article also eliminated the election of a superintendent of public instruction, an office whose elective status had been a questionable provision in 1870. Instead, the convention created a state board of education which would appoint a chief state school officer and executive officer for the board. The delegates showed some evidence of a desire for flexibility in the constitution by creating this state board. The number of its members, their qualifications, terms of office, and manner of selection were left to the legislature to determine. The governor did receive more authority in the legislative process with two new veto powers: an amendatory veto to correct technical defects in legislation, and a reduction veto to reduce the amount appropriated for an item.

The Legislative Committee disregarded the possibilities of such structural changes as reducing the number of legislators. In fact, the number of senators was increased by one. A proposal for a unicameral legislature was made, but not seriously considered. The convention did agree that a repetition of the at-large election of representatives in 1964 had to be avoided. The new apportionment provision, therefore, eliminated the at-large election. A commission would still be appointed if the legislature failed to apportion, but if the commission also became deadlocked, the state supreme court would submit the names of two persons, not of the same political party, to the secretary of state. One name would be drawn by lot, and that person would serve on the commission as a tie breaker.

The article on local government, on the other hand, provided the opportunity for substantive change, depending on its interpretation in the courts and on the use made of it by local governmental units. John Parkhurst chaired the Committee on Local Government which carefully constructed a new concept of local government for Illinois, although last-minute negotiations for Democratic support changed the original plan somewhat. The local government article reversed the doctrine that local governmental units had only the power expressly granted to them by state statute. Every city in Illinois over twenty-five thousand would automatically have full home rule power, as would every county which elected a chief executive officer. Cities under twenty-five thousand could obtain home rule power by referendum. All powers would go to these units unless specifically prohibited by the constitution, or preempted by the state legislature. Preemption would determine in part how much power the localities would actually have; otherwise, in Parkhurst's words, "the opportunity for innovation and diversity of solutions at the local level is practically unlimited."[27]

The revenue article accomplished much less change than the delegates might have expected at the time of the convention call. This was undoubtedly fortunate from the standpoint of the convention's success, for the failure of seven proposed revenue amendments in the twentieth century was an indication that Illinois voters could not agree on adequate revenue provisions for the state. However, by the time the delegates convened, events outside the convention had already done much to decide the issue. The Seventy-sixth General Assembly passed a flat-rate income tax, with a $2\frac{1}{2}$ percent rate for individuals and a 4 percent rate for corporations. This act was upheld the same year, 1969, by the state supreme court in *Thorpe* v. *Mahin*. In its decision the court specifically disavowed the *Bachrach* v. *Nelson* statement of 1932 that the General Assembly was limited to property taxes, occupation taxes, and franchise or privilege taxes. Their decision seemed to leave no bounds on the General Assembly's power to tax "in such manner as may be consistent with the principles of taxation fixed in this constitution."[28] Leading sentiment in the convention, particularly among representatives of business interests, therefore favored placing some restrictions on this taxing power. This goal was successful. A graduated income tax was prohibited, and corporations could be taxed at a rate higher than the rate on individuals but not in excess of an 8 to 5 ratio, the ratio in effect in 1969. Although labor groups objected to these restrictions, as did political scientists who preferred the abolition of the article altogether, the revenue article as adopted was a pragmatic attempt to alleviate fears of business and other groups of an unlimited taxing power. Chicago Democrats accepted the article largely because it authorized the classification of real estate in Cook and other counties over two hundred thousand population, which Chicago felt was essential to its financial stability.

Members of the Committee on Suffrage and Elections were deeply conscious of the necessity for public approval of their work. The

[27] John Parkhurst, "Local Government," *Illinois Constitutional Convention Summary* no. 32 (September 3, 1970), p. 11.
[28] Glenn W. Fisher, *Taxes and Politics: A Study of Illinois Public Finance* (Urbana: University of Illinois Press, 1969), p. 296.

suffrage article eased residency requirements for voters in recognition of the increased mobility of the population, and established a state board of elections for more uniform election procedures and inspections. However, despite extensive testimony from civic, business, labor, political, and educational leaders and organizations overwhelmingly in favor of lowering the voting age from twenty-one to eighteen, the committee decided that an issue so volatile and so susceptible to voter opposition should be submitted separately.[29] The committee's article on constitutional revision, however, went further than ever before in Illinois in realizing the twentieth-century goal of a flexible constitution. Both the amendment process and the requirements for calling a constitutional convention were liberalized. The article lowered to three-fifths the number of legislators needed to propose an amendment or a convention, and provided that a convention should be called or an amendment approved if either three-fifths of those voting on the issue or a majority voting at the election approved. The delegates also added a provision for automatic submission of the question of a convention call to popular referendum at least once every twenty years. Another new provision authorized popular initiative for changes in structural and procedural subjects in the legislative article.

SUBMISSION TO THE VOTERS

The convention adjourned on September 3, 1970, in an atmosphere of "relief, patriotism, and a sense of achievement."[30] Witwer's closing address reminded the delegates that "the Sixth Illinois Constitutional Convention is a test in microcosm of our national will to continue as one of history's great nations and civilizations." Looking ahead to the constitutional referendum on December 15, he suggested that citizens should ask themselves, "Is the Constitution of 1970 superior to the Constitution of 1870, [and] relevant to the problems of our State?"[31] Witwer's answer, and that of most of the delegates, was yes. A few, however, promised to go home and campaign against

[29] Peter Tomei, "Articles III and XIV and Separate Question No. 4 —Suffrage, Elections and Constitutional Revision," *Chicago Bar Record,* 52 (November 1970):71–76.
[30] *Chicago Today,* September 4, 1970.
[31] *Verbatim Transcripts,* September 3, 1970.

the constitution's passage. Two delegates refused to sign the document, Paul Elward because of his cautious approach to revision, and Thomas Kelleghan because the document had been written by "radicals."[32] John Alexander did sign the constitution, but immediately declared his opposition to its revenue restrictions, its refusal to incorporate eighteen-year-old voting and single-member House districts into the body of the document, and other defects.[33]

Despite these objections, however, few groups in the state opposed the constitution. Governor Ogilvie and the Republican organization endorsed it, as did U.S. senators Charles Percy and Adlai Stevenson. Mayor Daley and the Cook County Democratic organization waited until November 30 with their decision, and then gave the constitution their approval. Chicago Democrats were unhappy about submitting the election of judges to a popular vote, and campaigned more vigorously on this issue than on approval of the constitution. Still, Daley's support for the document was an important factor in its approval. The mayor had long been involved in constitutional reform, and for that reason may have been favorably disposed towards the new constitution. Also, the home rule provision and the classification of real estate in the revenue article filled definite Cook County needs.

Illinois educators and civic leaders who had worked long and hard in the constitutional revision field appeared satisfied with the new document. A spokeswoman for the League of Women Voters called it an "amazing document for 1970," particularly praising the bill of rights. The chairman of the Independent Voters of Illinois called it a "giant step forward." Other groups pledging official support included the Illinois State Chamber of Commerce, the Illinois Agricultural Association, the Illinois Bar Association, the Chicago Bar Association, and the Illinois Municipal League.[34]

James Kemp and William Lennon successfully urged the Illinois AFL-CIO to oppose the constitution because of its income tax restrictions and the possibility that cumulative voting would be abolished.[35] Labor's opposition, however, remained largely on the officer

[32] *Peoria Journal Star,* September 4, 1970.

[33] *Alton Evening Telegraph,* September 3, 1970.

[34] *Chicago Daily News,* September 2, 1970; *Chicago Sun-Times,* September 30, 1970; *Chicago Tribune,* October 8, 1970.

[35] *Chicago Sun-Times,* September 23, 1970.

level; rank and file labor members did not put on a strong campaign against the constitution. Opposing groups included coroners' and county clerks' associations, but the most vigorous opposition campaign was waged by the Save Our Suburbs group, renamed "Save Our State." In their literature against the constitution this group emphasized the fact that the new constitution would result in more taxes. Curiously, Save Our State ignored the sweeping bill of rights provision on open housing and employment. A campaign against this provision might have had a stronger appeal.

The press gave the proposed constitution strong and decisive support. All of Chicago's major newspapers supported it, the *Tribune* coming out with a signed front-page publisher's editorial the Sunday before election. Most downstate newspapers also kept the constitution before the voters with informational articles as well as editorials. Also extremely important for the constitution vote were the campaigns waged in behalf of two of the separately-submitted proposals. Several convention delegates, the convention's counsel to the legislative committee, and other civic leaders organized to promote Option 1-B, the choice of single-member districts for the election of representatives. They argued that cumulative voting was confusing to voters, stifled real party competition, and worked against representation of blacks and other minorities as well as minority political parties.[36] The most vigorous campaign, however, was waged for Option 2-B, merit selection of judges. The Committee for Merit Selection, backed by lawyers throughout the state, the Republican party, and civic groups such as the League of Women Voters, used a comprehensive precinct organization strategy in Cook County, attacking the suburban area heavily. The judicial question brought out a heavy vote in the county on both sides of the issue, and proponents of both sides recommended a favorable vote on the constitution itself.[37]

The constitution was approved on December 15 by a vote of 1,122,425 to 838,168. Cumulative voting was retained by a 1,031,-241 to 749,909 vote. Cook County's 280,000 plurality on the issue

[36] Citizens for Single-Member Districts, *Option 1-B: The Merits of Single-Member Legislative Districts*, pp. 6–12.

[37] This account of election results draws heavily on JoAnna M. Watson, "Analysis of the Vote at the Election for the 1970 Illinois Constitution," *Illinois Government* 34 (February 1971).

was enough to overcome wide geographic support for single-member districts. Voters also retained the election of judges, 1,013,559 to 867,230. The merit selection campaign in Cook County succeeded in neutralizing the heavy urban Democratic vote, but merit selection lost downstate. Voters also defeated the separately submitted propositions to abolish the death penalty and to lower the voting age to eighteen.

As in many previous constitutional elections, Cook County's majority was decisive in obtaining a favorable vote for the constitution. Its plurality of 350,000 votes overcame a negative vote by seventy-two downstate counties. Twice as many registered Chicago area voters turned out as downstate voters. Even though Illinois voter approval was not widespread geographically, the thirty counties which supported the constitution represented over 75 percent of the state's population.

The vote was light: 37 percent of the voting population of Illinois took part in the referendum, and 55.5 percent of these voted for the new constitution. This was hardly an overwhelming mandate, but it was a vote of approval, most significant when compared to the pattern in other states. Three other attempts at constitutional revision, in Arkansas, Idaho, and Oregon, were defeated in 1970. Those who had worked to bring about a new constitution for Illinois pondered the number of favorable circumstances which had to be combined to accomplish this vote of approval in their state.

The approved 1970 constitution would now provide the basic precepts for government in Illinois. As with past constitutions, though, its effect would depend on legislative implementation, judicial interpretations, and public demands on state government. These factors would determine the impact of constitutional change on the government and citizens of Illinois.

Bibliography

BOOKS, ARTICLES, AND PAMPHLETS

Anthony, Elliott. *The Constitutional History of Illinois*. Chicago: Chicago Legal News Print, 1891.

Bateman, Newton, ed. *Historical Encyclopedia of Illinois*. 2 vols. Chicago: Munsell Publishing Co., 1900.

Blair, George. "The Adoption of Cumulative Voting in Illinois." *Journal of the Illinois State Historical Society* 47 (1954).

Bogart, Ernest L. and John M. Mathews. *The Modern Commonwealth, 1893–1918*. Vol. 5 of The Centennial History of Illinois. Springfield: Illinois Centennial Commission, 1920.

————, and Charles M. Thompson. *The Industrial State, 1870–1893*. Vol. 4 of The Centennial History of Illinois. Chicago: Illinois Centennial Commission, 1922.

Braden, George D. and Rubin G. Cohn. *The Illinois Constitution: An Annotated and Comparative Analysis*. Urbana: Institute of Government and Public Affairs, University of Illinois, 1969.

Brown, Charles LeRoy. "Possibility of Illinois Being Divided into Two States." *Illinois Law Review* 7 (1912):30–41.

Buck, Solon J. *Illinois in 1818*. 2d ed. rev. Urbana: University of Illinois Press, 1967.

Buenker, John D. "Urban Immigrant Lawmakers and Progressive Reform in Illinois." In *Essays in Illinois History in Honor of Glenn Huron Seymour*, edited by Donald F. Tingley. Carbondale: Southern Illinois University Press, 1968.

Chandler, Henry P. "Thoughts on Constitution-Making Suggested by the Experience of Illinois." *University of Pennsylvania Law Review* 71 (1923): 218–28.

Chicago Bureau of Public Efficiency. *The Proposed New Constitution for Illinois*. Chicago, 1922.

————. *Shall the Proposed New Constitution Be Adopted? Vote Yes.* Chicago, 1922.

Citizens for Single-Member Districts. *Option 1B: The Merits of Single-Member Legislative Districts.*

Cole, Arthur C. *The Era of the Civil War, 1848–1870.* Vol. 3 of The Centennial History of Illinois. Chicago: Illinois Centennial Commission, 1922.

Cole, Arthur C., ed. *The Constitutional Debates of 1847. Collections of the Illinois State Historical Library* 14. Springfield, 1919.

Constitutional Convention Campaign Committee of Illinois. *Why Illinois Needs a New Constitution.* Springfield, 1918.

Dickerson, Oliver M. *The Illinois Constitutional Convention of 1862.* University of Illinois Studies in the Social Sciences, vol. 1, no. 9. Urbana, 1905.

Dunne, Edward F. *Illinois: The Heart of the Nation.* 5 vols. Chicago: The Lewis Publishing Co., 1933.

Elder, Ann H. and Glenn W. Fisher. *An Attempt to Amend the Illinois Constitution: A Study in Politics and Taxation.* Urbana: Institute of Government and Public Affairs, University of Illinois, 1969.

Elson, Alex. "Constitutional Revision and Reorganization of the General Assembly." *Illinois Law Review* 33 (1938):19–20.

Fisher, Glenn W. *Taxes and Politics: A Study in Illinois Public Finance.* Urbana: University of Illinois Press, 1969.

Ford, Thomas. *History of Illinois from Its Commencement as a State in 1818 to 1847.* Chicago: S. C. Griggs & Co., 1854.

"The Four Constitutional Conventions of the State of Illinois." *Journal of the Illinois State Historical Society* 11 (1918).

Gove, Samuel K. and Victoria Ranney, ed. *Con-Con: Issues for the Illinois Constitutional Convention.* Urbana: University of Illinois Press, 1970.

Haig, Robert M. *A History of the General Property Tax in Illinois.* University of Illinois Studies in the Social Sciences, vol. 3, nos. 1 and 2. Urbana, 1914.

Hutchinson, William T. *Lowden of Illinois: The Life of Frank O. Lowden.* 2 vols. Chicago: University of Chicago Press, 1957.

Kitsos, Thomas R. "Constitutional Amendments and the Voter, 1952–1966." Commission Papers of the Institute of Government and Public Affairs, University of Illinois. Urbana, 1968.

————, and Joseph P. Pisciotte. *A Guide to Illinois Constitutional Revision: The 1969 Constitutional Convention.* Urbana: Institute of Government and Public Affairs, University of Illinois, 1969.

Lavery, Urban A. "Status of the Illinois Constitutional Convention." *Illinois Law Review* 16 (1921–22):196–206.

Pease, Theodore C. *The Frontier State, 1818–1848.* Vol. 2 of The Centennial History of Illinois. Springfield: Illinois Centennial Commission, 1918.

————. *The Story of Illinois.* 3d ed. rev. by Marguerite Jenison Pease. Chicago: University of Chicago Press, 1965.

Pease, Theodore C., ed. *Illinois Election Returns, 1818–1848. Collections of the Illinois State Historical Library* 18. Springfield, 1923.

Pierce, Bessie L. *History of Chicago.* Vol. 2, *From Town to City, 1848–1871.* New York: Alfred A. Knopf, 1940.

Pisciotte, Joseph P. "How Illinois Did It." *National Civic Review* 58 (1969): 291–96.

Pooley, William V. *Settlement in Illinois from 1830 to 1850.* Reprinted from the *Bulletin of the University of Wisconsin,* History Series, 1 (1908).

Sears, Kenneth C. "Constitutional Revision in Illinois." *Illinois Law Review* 33 (1938):2–14.

———. "Voting on Constitutional Conventions and Amendments." *University of Chicago Law Review* 2 (1935):612–18.

———, and Charles V. Laughlin. "A Study in Constitutional Rigidity." *University of Chicago Law Review* 11 (1943):374–442.

Shankman, Arnold. "Partisan Conflicts, 1839–1841, and the Illinois Constitution." *Journal of the Illinois State Historical Society* 63 (1970):337–67.

Steiner, Gilbert Y. and Samuel K. Gove. *Legislative Politics in Illinois.* Urbana: University of Illinois Press, 1960.

Stevenson, Adlai E. "The Constitutional Conventions and Constitutions of Illinois." *Transactions of the Illinois State Historical Society* (1903), pp. 16–30.

Tomei, Peter A. "How Not to Hold a Constitutional Convention." *Chicago Bar Record* 49 (1968):179–90.

Verlie, Emil J., ed. *Illinois Constitutions. Collections of the Illinois State Historical Library* 13. Springfield, 1919.

Washburne, Elihu B. *Sketch of Edward Coles, Second Governor of Illinois and of the Slavery Struggle of 1823–1824.* Chicago: Jansen, McClurg & Co., 1882.

Watson, JoAnna M. "Analysis of the Vote at the Election for the 1970 Illinois Constitution." *Illinois Government* 34 (1970).

Wish, Harvey. "Altgeld and the Progressive Tradition." *American Historical Review* 46 (1940):813–31.

Witwer, Samuel. "The Illinois Constitution and the Courts." *University of Chicago Law Review* 15 (1947):53–77.

PUBLIC DOCUMENTS

Constitution of the State of Illinois and the United States. Springfield, 1967.

Debates and Proceedings of the Constitutional Convention of the State of Illinois Convened at the City of Springfield, Tuesday, December 13, 1869. 2 vols. Springfield, 1870.

Delegates' Manual of the Fifth Constitutional Convention of the State of Illinois, 1920. Edited by B. H. McCann. Springfield, 1920.

Illinois Blue Book. 1917–18, 1923–24.

Illinois Constitutional Convention Summary. Published weekly from January

17, 1970, to September 3, 1970, for the Constitutional Convention by the Illinois Legislative Council. Springfield.

Illinois. Constitution Study Commission. *Report Submitted to the 75th General Assembly.* February 1967.

——. House. *Journal.* 1893, 1917.

——. Legislative Reference Bureau. *The Constitution of Illinois.* Springfield, 1934.

——. Legislative Reference Bureau. *Constitution of the State of Illinois, Annotated.* Springfield, 1919.

——. Legislative Reference Bureau. *Constitutional Conventions in Illinois.* 2d ed. Springfield, 1919.

——. Legislative Reference Bureau. *General Statement of Work of Legislative Reference Bureau.* Springfield, 1919.

——. Secretary of State. Edward Rummell, comp. *The Illinois Hand-Book of Information for the Year 1870.* Springfield, 1870.

——. Senate. *Journal.* 1867, 1869, 1899, 1917, 1951.

Illinois Legislative Council. "Amending the Illinois Constitution." Memorandum 1–151. Springfield, March 1950.

——. *Constitutional Revision in Illinois.* Publication 85. Springfield, 1947.

——. *Legislative Apportionment in Illinois.* Publication 112. Springfield, 1952.

Illinois State Library. *The Constitution of Illinois: A Selective Bibliography.* Edited by Charlotte B. Stillwell and Stanley E. Adams. Springfield, 1970.

Journal of the Constitutional Convention, 1920–22, of the State of Illinois. Springfield, 1922.

Journal of the Constitutional Convention of the State of Illinois Convened at Springfield, January 7, 1862. Springfield, 1862.

Journal of the Convention (Kaskaskia, Ill., 1818), reprinted in the *Journal of the Illinois State Historical Society* 6 (1913):327–424.

Journal of the Convention Assembled at Springfield, June 7, 1847. Springfield, 1847.

Laws of Illinois. 1847, 1861, 1867, 1869, 1897, 1919, 1949, 1969.

Proceedings of the Constitutional Convention of the State of Illinois Convened January 6, 1920. 5 vols. Springfield, 1920–22.

The Proposed New Constitution of Illinois, 1922, with Explanatory Notes and Address to the People. Springfield, 1922.

Sixth Illinois Constitutional Convention. *Record of Proceedings: Verbatim Transcripts* (1969–1970).

U.S. Bureau of the Census. *Statistical View of the United States:...A Compendium of the Seventh Census.* 1850.

——. Bureau of the Census. *A Compendium of the Ninth Census of the United States.* 1870.

——. Bureau of the Census. *Thirteenth Census.* 1910.

——. Bureau of the Census. *Fourteenth Census.* 1920.

————. Congress. *Annals of Congress.* 15th Cong., 2d sess., 1818.
————. Congress. House. *Journal.* 15th Cong., 2d sess., 1818.
————. Congress. Senate. *Journal.* 15th Cong., 2d sess., 1818.

UNPUBLISHED MATERIALS

Hanson, Earl T. "The Chicago-Downstate Problem as Shown by the Illinois Constitutional Convention of 1920–1922." Master's thesis, University of Illinois, 1939.

Illinois. Official Election Returns. November 24, 1851, November 4, 1856, November 6, 1860, and June 17, 1862. State Archives. Springfield.

Thompson, William. "Illinois Constitutions." Ph.D. dissertation, University of Illinois, 1960.

Urbana. Illinois Historical Survey. Transcripts of Jesse W. Fell papers.

Urbana. Illinois Historical Survey. Lyman Trumbull papers.

Index